AFTER THE DELUGE

English Society Between the Wars

WORLD OUTLOOK 1900–1965: A Study Series

General Editor:

M. E. Bryant, Lecturer in the Teaching of History,
University of London Institute of Education

CLASS WORK BOOK by M. E. Bryant and Giles Ecclestone

Study books:

After the Deluge
ENGLISH SOCIETY BETWEEN THE WARS

John Standen, M.A.
Senior Lecturer in History
Gipsy Hill College of Education

Illustrated by
C. W. BACON
M.S.I.A.

FABER AND FABER
24 Russell Square, London

First published in 1969
by Faber and Faber Limited
24 Russell Square London WC1
Printed in Great Britain by
R. MacLehose and Company Limited
The University Press, Glasgow

SBN 571 08890 2

918259

942.083   14.10.69

Contents

Illustrations

LIST AND SOURCES

Acknowledgements

Acknowledgements are made to Mr. George Sassoon for permission to include extracts from 'They' and 'Suicide in the Trenches' by Siegfried Sassoon from *Collected Poems* (Faber); to Chappell & Co. Ltd. for permission to include part of 'The Party's Over Now' from *The Lyrics of Noël Coward* published by Heinemann Ltd, (Copyright 1932 by Chappell & Co. Ltd.); to David Higham Associates Ltd. for permission to include, 'The Almighty Cannot Bear to See' and 'Mother's Advice and Father's Fears' by Jacques Reval (James Laver) from *Between the Wars* by James Laver (Vista Books), for the extract from 'Aubade' by Edith Sitwell from *Collected Poems* (Macmillan) and extracts from *Modern England* by C. Hamilton (Dent); to Hutchinson Publishing Group Ltd. for extracts from *Reminiscences* by The Marchioness Curzon of Kedleston; to the David Low Trustees for extracts from David Low's *Autobiography* (Michael Joseph); to The Joseph Rowntree Charitable Trust for extracts from *Poverty and Progress* by B. S. Rowntree (Longmans); to Rupert Hart-Davis Ltd. for the extract from *The Light of Common Day* by D. Cooper; to Faber & Faber Ltd. for the extract from 'Spain 1937' by W. H. Auden from *Collected Shorter Poems 1930–1944* and the extract from 'Moving through the silent crowd' by Stephen Spender from *Collected Poems*.

Using This Book

Studying history is rather like using a cine-camera intelligently. To interpret a drama, to explore a scene, the cameraman uses distant shots, close-ups, different angles, he mixes darkness and light, stillness and speed. The historian must do much the same, for he too is trying to get details and perspective to come together.

This series, *World Outlook, 1900–1965*, tries to give a perspective picture of twentieth-century world history, and this book, *After the Deluge*, brings the camera closer down to focus on the twenty bleak years in England after the First World War, which had seemed like the flood which destroyed the world in the beginning of time. The writer uses many angles to explore those years — he looks at them through the eyes of the artist, the poor, the frightened, the disillusioned, the light-hearted, the serious-minded.

To get the best out of this view, you could as it were work *with* the camera, exploring the close-ups, letting the shadows and the high-lights show up the features of people and places. Get an eye for detail and points of view. Study your local war memorial. What can you learn from the various styles in which memorials were built? What kind of symbols expressed sorrow and desolation?

Make anthologies or albums, or arrange concerts to show how artists (great and not-so-great) reacted to the events of these times. Find out what happened in the 'Depression' in your district. What new industries were developed? How did your shopping centre change? Could you reconstruct some of the activities of your branch of the League of Nations Union, using local newspapers and the memories of members? You could even ask apparently trivial questions such as: What was the significance for world history of a tin of Heinz Baked Beans? You might be surprised at the answers.

You will find that in these twenty years in England are concentrated many of the problems which have shaped the twentieth-century world. This close-up view must be placed in perspective. Moving the camera back, a distant view shows that the divisions and violence and miseries between the Wars were a continuation of those which caused the First War. By 1914 the world had already become one huge market for food and raw materials (that is where the tin of baked beans fits in). But it had not developed any political, international, machinery for dealing with clashes that arose because of this (hence the war memorial). The War hastened the break-up of old ideas and institutions (your albums, anthologies, concerts show this). At last in 1919 the League of Nations was set up (but was your local branch widely supported and realistic in its views?) The League was still very much a European affair. Could Europe solve her own problems? (Why were men in your district unemployed?) Other books in this series give help with other parts of the world and the *Embattled Peace* discusses the international scene. The *World Outlook Class Work-Book* gives suggestions for organizing studies into what might be called the finished film — a picture of twenty very significant years.

MARGARET BRYANT

1. Armistice Day 1918. Crowds gather outside Buckingham
Palace, cheering and singing

I

The War is Over

On 11th November 1918 a small crowd, which had gathered
outside Buckingham Palace to watch the changing of the guard,
heard a rumour that the war was over, and at 11 a.m. a type-
written copy of the Prime Minister's announcement of the end
of fighting was hung up outside the railings. The news spread.
People began to converge on the Mall. The Victoria memorial
was soon crowded with a cheering throng and King George
and Queen Mary came out onto the balcony. Helped by the
band of the Irish Guards, the crowd sang the National Anthem
and 'Rule Britannia', and at lunch time the King appeared
again and spoke: 'With you I rejoice and thank God for the
victories which the Allied Armies have won, bringing hostilities
to an end and peace within sight.' The crowd burst into song
once more and continued with 'Auld Lang Syne', 'Tipperary',
'Keep the Home Fires Burning', 'Land of Hope and Glory' and
the American, Belgian and French national anthems.

At 3 p.m. the King and Queen drove through the West End
and the City of London, and the next day they attended a
thanksgiving service at St. Paul's. There thousands joined in
'Praise, my soul, the King of Heaven' and for the first time sang
the new tune by Vaughan Williams to 'For All the Saints'. Its
sturdy, marching rhythm and broad, confident tune might be
thought particularly suitable for a time when Britain needed to
stride confidently into the post-war world.

People could certainly soon forget some of the war-time
conditions. The Board of Trade's propaganda to persuade
housewives to start fires with the previous day's cinders — 'The
coal you go without is forging the key to victory' — was
abandoned. Hotels, restaurants, clubs and theatres were

allowed to be heated and lighted; the blackout around the street lights was removed; firework displays were no longer prohibited; and restrictions on the ringing of bells and the chiming of public clocks ended.

2. King George V and Queen Mary attended the Thanksgiving Service at St. Paul's Cathedral

The day named for the official peace celebrations was 7th December. This gave time for the arrangements to be made and for some troops to return, but the majority of soldiers who had known active service were to be welcomed later. In fact the celebrations were stretched out over a period during which it would have been impossible in any circumstances to keep up enthusiasm and a mood of rejoicing, especially when so many families had suffered immense personal loss during the war.[1] The Lord Mayor's Procession that year took the form of a

[1] See Katharine Moore, *Family Fortunes*.

war display with British and foreign troops and captured German guns. Taking place early in November, it was a popular success. By the end of the month the public celebrations and private 'peace parties' had become rather jaded, for the problems of peace were already looming large.

In the early autumn of 1918 as the war had drawn to a close, people began to wonder what life would be like after the war. *The Times* asked: 'How are we to pass from war conditions to peace conditions?' And this was certainly a question of great importance and one which was never completely solved. During the war the British people had seemed united by the war effort. Such unity had not been present before 1914.[1] Could unity outlive the war? It seemed not, for even before 1918 there had been some criticism of the very war which for a time had brought unity.

One writer had put his doubts and fears like this: 'Sometimes I am swept away with admiration for all the heroism of the War or by some particularly noble self-sacrifice and think it is really all worthwhile. Then — and more frequently — I remember that this war has let loose in the world not only barbarities, butcheries and crimes, but lies, lies, lies — hypocrisies, deceits, ignoble desire for self-aggrandizement, self-preservation — such as no one ever dreamed existed. . . . The war is everything: it is noble, filthy, great, petty, degrading, inspiring, ridiculous, glorious, mad, bad, hopeless, yet full of hope. I don't know what to think about it. We are like a nest of frightened ants when someone lifts the stone. That is the world just now.'[2] It is hardly surprising that people felt despondent, for the war had been long instead of short as everyone had expected, and, when they looked back on the war, it seemed futile and to have achieved nothing. Once the war was over many questions and problems were bound to come out into the open: the division between those who had fought in the war and those who had stayed at home became apparent. This cleavage in society was to form one of the

[1] See John Standen, *The Edwardians* and Dennis Starkings, *British Democracy in the Twentieth Century.*

[2] *Barbellion's Diary* quoted in A. Ponsonby, *English Diaries* (Methuen, 1923), p. 441.

problems of the inter-war years and helped to smash any unity which remained in England after the war.

Let one of those who fought in the war, the young soldier poet, Siegfried Sassoon, who had been invalided out of the war but who had returned to the battle-front, speak for his generation and tell us how he felt. He realized that after the war soldiers would fit ill into English life:

> 'We're none of us the same,' the boys reply.
> 'For George lost both his legs; and Bill's stone blind;
> Poor Jim's shot through the lungs and like to die;
> And Bert's gone syphilitic: you'll not find
> A chap who's served that hasn't found some change.'

When it came to peace celebrations, Sassoon, knowing the horrors of war, found himself out of sympathy with others who had not fought. 'Now it so happened that my friend and I were the only members of the party who had seen any active service, while two of the others were of an age which suggested that they might likewise have done so, had their now exuberant patriotism prompted them to adventure. Towards the end of an excellent dinner this unfortunate cleavage became conspicuous. We were involved in an inimical argument with a youngish gentleman whose war services . . . had been devoted to assisting on the Central Liquor Control Board. Our moral advantage over him made the situation awkward. It was, no doubt, the wrong moment for me to exclaim that the War had been a loathsome tragedy and that all this flag-waving couldn't alter it; but he wasn't in

3. A village war memorial

a position to support the opposite view with fine phrases. We left the house extremely unpopular, and as we walked away I told my friend that his Armistice night entertainment had been a ruddy washout.'

In other writings Sassoon hit out at the misery of the war which not all had suffered and which was now being treated as something heroic by the peace celebrations:

> You smug-faced crowds with kindling eye
> Who cheer when soldier lads march by
> Sneak home and pray you'll never know
> The hell where youth and laughter go.

The bitterness against the war had arisen gradually since 1914 as can be seen from war poets such as Wilfred Owen and Sassoon. Such poets were able to express their horror of war, and their compassion for those who suffered, in poems which were expressed in everyday language of a type far removed from the poetry of pre-war and early wartime Britain. In the same way war painters had altered their style in depicting war scenes. Artists such as Paul Nash and Stanley Spencer painted cubist and surrealist pictures which emphasized the loathsomeness of war. The extreme wretchedness of the soldiers' lives meant that the only things they could look forward to were the return of peace and life in England — the 'land fit for heroes' which politicians promised.

Soldiers therefore developed two attitudes. They wanted to lead the peaceful life in England which they remembered — or imagined they remembered — from pre-war days. This was shown in a widespread desire to get back to 'normalcy' as soon as possible and to forget the horrors of war. In one way it led to idealizing English life and countryside. Francis Ledwidge, killed in 1917, expressed this nostalgia in poems which already sounded old-fashioned:

> When the war is over I shall take
> My lute a-down and sing again
> Songs of the whispering things amongst the brake,
> And those I love shall know them by their strain.

Their airs shall be the blackbird's twilight song,
Their words shall be all flowers with fresh dews hoar,
But it is lonely now in winter long,
And, God! to hear the blackbird sing once more.[1]

This view was widely shared by many civilians in England, especially the ruling class, although their ideas on 'normalcy' varied greatly. But conditions had changed and it was impossible to go back to a previous way of life. As the cartoonist, Low, said: 'After the war everybody had wanted Peace everlasting ... but war was not to be abolished just by throwing aside one's rifle into a ditch and walking off the battlefield. Peace had to be organized.'[2]

Secondly, those returning from active service wanted to live in an England which had progressed and which would provide better conditions than previously. This was in many respects directly opposed to the return to the kind of normalcy desired by many civilians, and in actual fact a soldier found that he returned to a slightly worse world than he had lived in during pre-war days — worse because he felt cut-off from those who had remained at home and because wartime promises of better conditions were not fulfilled. Was it any wonder that soldiers felt that they had been 'sold'? With the social distinctions of pre-war days still present in Britain, there was not even the comradeship that soldiers had experienced in the trenches. Soldiers returning from the front were struck by the old-fashioned divisions of society, as if the war had never taken place.

Britain, it seemed, had not changed enough; nor were many people willing to change; the soldiers had already changed too much. This is how Sassoon put it:

The Bishop tells us: 'When the boys come back
They will not be the same; for they'll have fought
In a just cause ...

. . . .

They have challenged Death and dared him face to face.'

[1] *The Complete Poems of Francis Ledwidge* (Herbert Jenkins).
[2] *Low's Autobiography* (Michael Joseph, 1956), p. 244.

Soldiers, although they were praised as heroes, were doomed to see their hopes for a fine future disappointed.

But the soldiers were not the only section of society who found that the war effort had hardly been worthwhile. There was scarcely a family in the country which had not suffered some personal loss during the war. Eight out of every twenty men in the armed forces had been killed and the total number of British soldiers and sailors dead was about 750,000.[1] Every town and village, every college and school, still gives testament to this in their lists of those killed, and the significance of the numbers can often be realized by comparing these lists with the much smaller lists for the Second World War. Nor had death been selective: it struck both high and low. Indeed it was among the highest of those who volunteered for service, especially the junior officers, that casualties were greatest. Thus it was that the young men of promise who were struck down became known as the 'lost generation'. In political life this meant that the old, traditional rulers of Britain carried on ruling the post-war world which they did not understand, for there were few to take over from them.

4. Siegfried Sassoon

They certainly did not understand Britain's economic plight. True, there was a post-war boom — this was one of the happier sides of the end of the war — when, for a while, wages almost

[1] For comparative figures of France, Britain and USA see Pauline Bloncourt, *The Embattled Peace 1919–1939*, Appendix C.

kept up with prices, and a better standard of living seemed available. But soon prices began to rise, especially after the government lifted war-time controls from industries without adequate planning. Wages soon lagged disastrously behind prices; there was a series of strikes and the boom ended towards the close of 1920. British people could not afford to buy goods; overseas markets were strictly limited by the effects of war; and the government had greatly restricted its own spending. British industries found themselves suffering from over-production for they had misjudged the markets for their goods. There was a quick cut-back in production. Unemployment rose, reaching two million in mid-1921.

What then had come of the promise of a land 'fit for our boys to live in'? The victors began to wonder more than ever what they had been fighting for. They soon learnt that Britain was still a country of deep social cleavages; now they were learning that it was in a state of economic turmoil which prevented them from earning their living. Soon they were to discover that the dole was what was fit for heroes. It is not surprising that deep cynicism was aroused in those who had suffered and that the end of the war was a prelude to one of the most disturbed periods of British history. Although there was peace, it was a time of the deepest disillusionment and bitter self-questioning: 'What am I? O God, nothing, less than nothing. . . . What right have I to live? Is it five million [who are dead], is it ten million, is it twenty million? What does the exact count matter? There they are, and we are responsible! . . . When I meet an unmarried man of my generation I want to shout at him: "How did you escape? How did you dodge it? What dirty trick did you play? Why are you not dead, trickster?" You the war dead, I think you died in vain, I think you died for nothing, for a blast of wind, a blather, a humbug, a newspaper stunt, a politician's ramp. But at least you died!'[1]

Such people, and there were many of them, might well agree with Sassoon's embittered comment:

'And the Bishop said: "The ways of God are strange." '

[1] R. Aldington, *Death of a Hero* (1929) quoted by J. Laver, *Between the Wars* (Vista Books, 1961), p. 22.

2

Society after the War

The war had caused upheavals in nearly every aspect of life in Britain. For soldiers war had meant mixing together in the fighting, while at home there had been a common bond in the desire to win the war. Scarcity of manpower meant that women played a greater part in the running of the country than ever before. These are some of the social effects of the war. The economy of the country had been affected too. Wartime demands had brought revolutionary development — many industries were both centrally controlled by the government and geared to the needs of war. Before getting back to normal economic life, decisions would have to be made to de-control industries and the necessary plans would have to be drawn up to return to peacetime production. There had also been changes in politics during the war. The wartime coalition Government under Lloyd George in some ways made the distinctions between parties less clear-cut and this situation was continued after the war when Lloyd George's supporters from all parties at the election of 1919 were issued with a 'coupon' to show the electorate whether they sympathized with the coalition government or not. This was the famous 'Coupon' election and it blurred party divisions still more, for Lloyd George's resulting Ministry was by no means wholly Liberal. No one knew whether the two traditional parties, the Conservatives and Liberals, would emerge from the war as the leading parties of the future. And what part would the small but vigorous Labour Party play in peacetime? We must therefore look at these social, economic and political changes caused by the war in more detail, for it was these changes that formed the background to the inter-war years.

Not quite everything had changed in society for we still had the same King as before the war. George V emerged from the war as a much-loved monarch who, with his consort, Queen Mary, had unstintingly carried out his duty. Together they helped provide some continuity in high society and leadership for the country, but almost inevitably they belonged more to the pre-war 1914 world rather than to the years after 1918. In a way this may have been a stabilizing factor in society, but it also meant that they, like the leaders of the political parties, were often out of sympathy with modern ways of life. King George could no more approve of his son's Friday to Sunday holidays — 'Damned weekends' he called them — than Queen Mary could appreciate the new-found freedom of women.

By far the most obvious of changes in society was the position of women. The part they had played in the war had liberated them from the stifling conventions of Victorian and Edwardian times which had made all but women of the lower class, or women prepared to rebel, lead lives which were as monotonous as they were useless. But during the war women had proved that in the absence of their menfolk they could do all the jobs considered suitable only for men. Clerical work in government departments and in private offices was largely taken over by women; they even entered the engineering trades; they formed a 'land army'; their importance in munitions factories can hardly be overestimated.

Taking part in such work not only made women more independent. Fewer were willing during and after the war to go into domestic service. For one thing wages were higher in industries and offices; for another, being a servant gave a woman much less free time than almost any other job. This decline in the number of servants had far-reaching effects on both the lower class which provided the servants and the upper class, which found it increasingly difficult to get — or afford — them. Low wages were no longer acceptable. In this way the war had helped to raise the social status of women. One commentator who saw women become free after the war has written of it in the following way: 'The war brought deliverance. Under the necessities of the time fashion gave way, and short-skirted uniforms, and even breeches, became familiar sights. Women, when they had once really tasted the joys of this deliverance, refused to be put back into the old costumes. . . . Skirts grew shorter and shorter, clothes grew more and more simple and convenient, and hair . . . was cut short. With one bound the young women of 1919 burst out from the hampering conventions and with their cigarettes, their motor-cars, their latch-keys, and their athletics they astonished and scandalized their elders.'[1]

5. Viscountess Astor, the first woman M.P., during a strenuous election campaign

After 1918 women could serve on juries and soon they were admitted to many professions, including law. At the same time they were granted full membership of Oxford University, but not of Cambridge until 1921. Higher education for women became much more general. As if in response to this — and partly to reward women for their war services when they had proved themselves reliable citizens — women over 30 were given the vote by the *Representation of the People Act (1918)*. The first woman M.P. was Lady Astor, elected the following year, but no other woman entered Parliament until Mrs. Wintringham in 1921. In fact the number of women M.P.s remained extremely small. This reflected the reluctance of the political parties to support women candidates, as well as the fact that the really go-ahead, independent women were still in a minority.

In some ways the new-found freedom of women showed

[1] R. Strachey, *The Cause* (1928) quoted in J. Laver, op. cit.

more obviously in dress and their general attitude to life and behaviour. As one observer has already told us, long dresses and large hats were no longer practical for a 'working girl'. Long hair, too, went out of fashion. It is helpful to keep an eye on fashion as it is a sign of more important changes. These changes in fashion were an outward sign of women's independence. At the end of the war it was considered daring if the skirt was short enough to display the ankle. Later much more than the knee was displayed, to the great distress of many people. In 1924 Birmingham waitresses were forbidden by their employers to wear short skirts, while the Archbishop of Naples declared that God's anger had been aroused by the immorality of short dresses, resulting in an earthquake at Amalfi. One person answered:

> The Almighty cannot bear to see
> The female leg above the knee.
> It simply isn't fit to show;
> He made it — so He ought to know.[1]

At the same time heels gradually got higher. Some daring women began to wear trousers in imitation of women land-workers. Blouses were loose fitting and shapeless. Women took to wearing men's woollen jumpers and pullovers. Gradually some of the outside distinctions between men and women began to disappear — it was all part of the way women showed that they were the equal of men and were doing many of the same jobs.

Clothes also showed women's new interests and activities. With ragtime and jazz had come the tremendous popularity of dancing. At first the dancing mania showed itself in the organization of dances for relief funds after the war, but soon dances were organized by all respectable, 'with-it' hostesses, and public dances were arranged in all large towns on most evenings. With admission as low as a shilling, the young of all classes could afford them. Tangos, foxtrots, one-steps, and the 'modern' waltz were taught and learnt avidly. Dancing was no longer the formal social activity where you literally kept your

[1] J. Laver (J. Reval), op. cit., p. 108.

partner at arm's length. The new modes did not go uncriticized. One clergyman maintained: 'If these up-to-date dances, described as the "latest craze", are within a hundred miles of all I hear about them, I should say that the morals of a pig-sty would be respectable in comparison.' Leaders of Church and State seemed to spend a great deal of time saying this sort of thing. The most notable performer was William Joynson-Hicks, who was Home Secretary from 1924 to 1929. 'Jix', as he was called, was a quite incredible person who was determined to clean up Britain, and prevent anyone enjoying himself in ways Jix did not understand. He had, therefore, plenty of scope.

To many it was still a scandal that women, perhaps un-chaperoned, should go to a public dance hall. It was rumoured that women were also going into public houses and bars — in York in 1936 the men and women at hotel bars were almost equal in number. It was even accepted that women smoked in public. Another scandal was the amount of make-up that they used. Slight colouring of the cheeks was no longer enough. The modern girl used rouge, lipstick, eye-shadow and eyebrow colouring. These are the obvious changes which gained notoriety after the war — changes which were the result of the underlying rejection of authority of the time. It is still the picture we usually have of the typical young women of the twenties — the 'Bright Young Things' as they were called:

> Mother's advice and Father's fears
> Alike are voted just a bore,
> There's Negro music in our ears
> The World is one huge dancing floor.
> We mean to tread the Primrose Path,
> In spite of Mr. Joynson-Hicks.
> We're People of the Aftermath,
> We're girls of 1926.
>
> In greedy haste, on pleasure bent
> We have no time to think, or feel,
> What need is there for sentiment
> Now we've invented **Sex Appeal**?

We've silken legs and scarlet lips,
We're young and hungry, wild and free.
Our waists are round about the hips,
Our skirts are well above the knee.

We've boyish busts and Eton crops,
We quiver to the saxophone,
Come, dance before the music stops,
And who can bear to be alone?
Come drink your gin, or sniff your 'snow',
Since Youth is brief, and Love has wings.
And Time will tarnish, e'er we know,
The brightness of the Bright Young Things.[1]

Such developments were felt to be expressive of women's new-found freedom, but it was not only women who felt freer in the years after 1918. Each section of society acted with greater freedom within itself, although the free attitude did little to break down class barriers. But these divisions were different from the divisions of pre-war times. In some ways the section that emerged triumphant from the First World War was 'business society', which was represented in politics by the Conservative leaders, Stanley Baldwin, a wealthy iron manufacturer, and the Chamberlain family, Birmingham industrialists. In business society in general there were many new faces, for fortunes had been made in wartime and war profiteers had entered and remained in 'society' after the war, sometimes mixing rather uneasily with the traditional aristocratic society of England. The aristocracy was increasingly on the defensive both socially and economically and was much less important than in pre-war days. In the post-war period it became more and more usual for the aristocracy to marry into business families and both sides found the result profitable. The House of Lords could still count on some prestige and it had the grace to welcome newly created peers warmly. In this way it strengthened itself. Yet there can be no doubt that the nobility was waning and there seemed to be no way round the increasing burden of taxation, particularly death duties.

[1] J. Laver, op. cit., p. 114.

At the side of business and aristocratic society, and in part over-lapping with both, was 'high society' — the 'Smart Set' made up of the 'Bright Young Things'. It was this group that gave the twenties their names — The Gay or Careless Twenties — and it was they who gave the inter-war years their popular image. We remember the Smart Set as typical of their day when really they were only a small section of society. The Smart Set's centre was Mayfair and their world was that portrayed in the plays of Noël Coward. Their aim was to have a good time, and in a way this sprang from the desire to get away from the horrors of war. There was often an element of 'escapism' in their frantic efforts to enjoy themselves, for they were frequently disillusioned and cynical — even about their own attempts to 'live it up'. One picture of this society is given in Evelyn Waugh's novel, *Vile Bodies*. A less exaggerated account is shown in the lyrics of Noël Coward.

6. Gertrude Lawrence in a number by Noël Coward called 'Parisian Pierrot'

The most usual thing to do was to go to parties: **'garden** parties on the cropped lawns of stately homes; studio bottle parties where the crush was so great that one had to move out into the street to lift one's elbow; music parties, fancy-dress parties, folk dance and ballet parties, sporting nights out. . . . Anything less than a hundred guests to a plain party was a quiet evening at home.'

The Marchioness Curzon gave parties that were as sumptious as those of pre-war days but with 'modern' entertainment. On one occasion she 'had a large number of guests for dinner, including the King and Queen of Spain, the Prince of Wales. . . . A big marquee had been built on the terrace overlooking the Mall, with a good floor for dancing. The Gobelin tapestry from Hackwood was hung round the walls of the marquee, and the beautiful silver chandeliers . . . were hung from the ceiling. . . . To enter the marquee guests had to descend three or four steps . . . on each side of [which] I had enormous blocks of ice covered with water lilies from Hackwood. . . . Ambrose's band played in the marquee, and the upstairs drawing room had been turned into another ballroom, where Cassano's band played.'

The Marchioness's parties were still fairly formal, although at one fancy dress ball she changed half-way through the evening and mingled unrecognized among her guests as a Negro parson: 'My face was blacked, I wore a skull cap to simulate baldness, a black suit and big masculine shoes.' Such a thing could never have happened before the war.

Usually parties and dances were far less formal — more exciting — none more than those of the press tycoon Lord Beaverbrook because of the different people who attended: 'Of all the parties Beaverbrook's took the cake for variety. Bankers, diplomats, peers, writers, artists, tycoons, film stars, Tories, Liberals and Socialists, Cabinet Ministers and trade union leaders.' There were wilder parties too. Parties which went on till dawn, although they did not meet with everyone's approval: 'Funny way to enjoy yourself, staying up all night when you don't 'ave to.' A continual round of parties eventually became dull, and high society's disillusionment came out into the open: they did not even enjoy doing what they wanted to do:

'Though we hate
Abominate
Each party we're invited to
  To stay out
  And dance about
Because we've nothing else to do.
Though every night
We start out bright
  And finish with a row
We've been so bored
Thank the Lord
  That the Party's over now!'[1]

In fact it was always necessary to invent new amusements —
or import them from America or the Continent. It was the
Smart Set that patronized the newly-opened night clubs and
restaurants of London. Night clubs, usually with cabaret, were
something new and exciting and were in constant danger from
police raids. The members of the Brighter London Society,
founded in 1922, helped to popularize the Kit-Kat Club, the 43
and the Silver Slipper. One of the owners, Mrs. Kate Meyrick,
spent a number of periods in gaol, after bribing a police
sergeant for many years to let her know when there was to be a
police raid. The six-pounds-a-week sergeant in question was
found to own a freehold house, a car and a safe containing
£12,000, which he maintained was the profit from selling rock
at the Wembley Exhibition on his day off. 'Jix', still Home
Secretary, and still trying to clean up London, got the sergeant 18
and Mrs. Meyrick 15 months hard labour. Nevertheless, three
of Mrs. Meyrick's daughters still married into the aristocracy.

Other more eccentric amusements helped to keep the Bright
Young Things from utter boredom: a hide-and-seek club at
Oxford; midnight treasure hunts in London; and constant
changes in popular dances, so that the Twinkle, Jog Trot and
Camel Walk soon gave way to the Charleston and Black
Bottom. In the Charleston decorum left dancing for all time
and it was regarded as immoral by the Vicar of Bristol: 'Any

[1] by Noël Coward

lover of the beautiful will die rather than be associated with the Charleston. It is neurotic! It is rotten! It stinks! Phew, open the windows.' Such wild and exaggerated reactions to any new

7. Jean Rai in the Charleston costume she wore to dance in *Frivolities*

activities were as typical of the Church as of 'Jix'. What such critics of new ways of life entirely failed to grasp was the moderation of the so-called rebels; there was nothing very extreme about most of them as we can see from the Wooster novels of P. G. Wodehouse.

Bertie Wooster, the young hero of *Carry on Jeeves*, wants to engage a new valet. The domestic agency send him Jeeves . . .

'I shall always remember the morning he came. It so happened that the night before I had been present at a rather cheery little supper, and I was feeling pretty rocky. On top of this I was trying to read a book Florence Craye had given me. She had been one of the house-party at Easeby, and two or three days before I left we had got engaged. I was due back at the end of the week, and I knew she would expect me to have finished the book by then. You see, she was particularly keen on boosting me up a bit nearer her own plane of intellect. She was a girl with a wonderful profile, but steeped to the gills in serious purpose. . . .'

While Bertie is trying to read *Types of Ethical Theory* through his hangover, Jeeves arrives for his interview.

' "I was sent by the agency, sir," he said. "I was given to understand that you required a valet."

'I'd have preferred an undertaker; but I told him to stagger in, and he floated noiselessly through the doorway like a healing zephyr. That impressed me from the start. He had a grave, sympathetic face, as if he, too, knew what it was to sup with the lads.

' "Excuse me, sir," he said gently.

'Then he seemed to flicker, and wasn't there any longer. I heard him moving about in the kitchen, and presently he came back with a glass on a tray.

' "If you would drink this, sir," he said, with a kind of bedside manner, rather like the royal doctor shooting the bracer into the sick prince. "It is a little preparation of my own invention. It is the Worcester Sauce that gives it its colour. The raw egg makes it nutritious. The red pepper gives it its bite. Gentlemen have told me they have found it extremely invigorating after a late evening."

'I would have clutched at anything that looked like a lifeline that morning. I swallowed the stuff. For a moment I felt as if somebody had touched off a bomb inside the old bean and was strolling down my throat with a lighted torch, and then everything seemed suddenly to get all right. The sun shone in through the window; birds twittered in the tree-tops; and, generally speaking, hope dawned once more.

' "You're engaged!" I said, as soon as I could say anything.'

But the great mass of the population belonged to none of these sections of society. They lived a far different life and although they were as disillusioned as the Smart Set, they certainly had more reason to be. Their lives were much influenced by mass entertainment, by advertising and by newspapers and, perhaps, most of all, by the BBC, which seemingly in the interests of peace and quiet helped to keep the masses amused and to provide the kind of informed but sober public of which people like Baldwin and even 'Jix' approved.

The public certainly had to be sober to listen to the wireless at first, for early crystal sets, selling at a few shillings, gave anything but good reception. If you could get a room to yourself and fiddle with the knobs for a while and find a comfortable way to wear your headphones, you might then hear voices or music dimly in the background of what sounded like a thunderstorm. But despite all this, broadcasting cast its spell: ' "Listening in" was a solemn ritual, like watching television in later years. . . . The wireless set was accepted as a

(*a*)

(*b*)

8. The crystal detector, (a) horizontal type and (b) vertical type

feature of the average house, and soon the coils, wires, loud-speaker and controls of the primitive sets were combined into one box or cabinet. Indoor aerials were installed in attics. . . . Schoolboys were the keenest amateurs. . . . To others the "magic box" remained a mystery. When the Archbishop of

Canterbury heard a wireless set for the first time, in March 1923, he asked if it were necessary to leave a window open'[1] — to let in the waves presumably.

With the arrival of broadcasting there also came problems, for it was obvious that the wireless could be used for propaganda unless it were controlled by some means or other. Two solutions were found: on the one hand if you wanted a wireless you had to buy a licence — one and a quarter million radio licences had been bought by 1924 — and on the other, the programmes broadcast were controlled by the British Broadcasting Company from 1922, the forerunner of the British Broadcasting Corporation which gained its royal charter as a corporation in 1926. This was the British answer to the problem of uncontrolled broadcasting — America, for instance, went a completely different way with broadcasting and advertising, a kind of propaganda, linked closely together. It was also both the strength and the weakness of broadcasting in England: the BBC had full powers which it used as a magnificent educative force, but there was, too, a real

9. Lord Reith

danger of a lack of breadth in outlook and puritanical limitations in the name of good taste or for the supposed public good.

The BBC was lucky in its director-general, John Reith, who, although perhaps over-serious-minded and lacking in lightness of touch, was convinced of the mission which the wireless had in the education of a right-thinking public. The BBC soon 'came to be regarded as an essential element in "the British way of life". . . . The English people, if judged by the BBC, were

[1] J. Montgomery, *The Twenties* (1957) quoted in J. Laver, op. cit., p. 59.

uniformly devout and kept to the middle of the road.'[1] This was just the kind of sober public that Baldwin and his political colleagues wanted and that, perhaps by accident, the BBC provided. It may also be significant that the radio could be used for political broadcasts, and that the politician who made the most effect with his relaxed and confident manner was Baldwin.

Regular news bulletins read in the 'standard English' spoken and spread by the BBC provided a framework for the programmes, often heard by over two and a half million households, for there were that number of licence holders as early as 1927. Probably three times as many people as licence holders 'listened in', though not, of course, to every programme. Classical music, in which sphere the BBC did some of its best educational work, inevitably had fewer listeners at first than more popular forms of music. Variety and concert parties, light orchestral music and military and dance bands had huge audiences and came to the top of the *Daily Mail* Gallup poll of programmes in 1927. What was important was the fact that the BBC persevered in its educational programmes and in catering for minority tastes, so that serious music, plays, talks and discussions became a normal part of broadcasting. At the same time the 'big' public could listen to The Savoy Orpheans, Paul Whiteman, Jack Payne and Henry Hall and hear the latest hits — 'Bye Bye Blackbird', 'I Wonder Where my Baby is Tonight', 'No foolin' ' and 'Ukelele Dream Girl'. The glamour of the wireless became very real to people who led ordinary lives. This was shown by the huge numbers who wrote for auditions to broadcast and the romance surrounding the idea of marrying an announcer. The unifying effect of the BBC was also important. As early as 1935 G. M. Trevelyan could write in *The Times* that 'broadcasting gives the whole country a common type of culture'.

Another powerful influence in mass entertainment was the cinema. In 1919 Northcliffe had explained, 'I had no notion what a topic of public conversation among all classes films have become,' and he began a weekly column of film criticism

[1] A. J. P. Taylor, *English History 1914–1945*, *Oxford History of England* V. 15 (Oxford University Press, 1965), p. 233.

in the *Daily Mail*. At first after the war people went to the silent films with some suspicion, but enjoyed the antics of Charlie Chaplin, Harold Lloyd, Buster Keaton and Felix the Cat. Westerns soon gained popularity and so did historical and romantic stories such as *The Sheikh*, starring Rudolph Valentino, and *Robin Hood* with Douglas Fairbanks (senior). Starring opposite them were the glamorous Mary Pickford, Gloria Swanson and Bebe Daniels. Cinemas grew larger and larger with the demands of the public, and to provide sound effects there were 'weird gadgets that looked like a lot of old dustbins and the entrails of a Ford; sirens for out-going steamers, bells for fire-engines, arrangements for imitating the gallop of horses, the smashing of crockery, the song of the nightingale, the crackling of fire, the roar of cannons, thunder, express trains, tornados, disappointed lovers, rhinoceri, chipmunks.'[1] Yet despite such makeshift arrangements and despite the appearance of stout ladies to sing songs that came from the mouth of the hero on the screen, silent films developed into an art-form in their own right. A special quality was needed in the acting of silent-film stars and the artistry of the greatest silent-film actors and directors still has its value today.

As the public became more sophisticated, criticism of silent films grew. In 1929 'talkies' were shown — the first with Al Jolson in *The Singing Fool*. Hollywood — originally a small village south of Los Angeles picked as a home by the producer, Carl Laemmle, who began the star system by giving up the anonymity of early silent-film actors — remained supreme in the production of talkies. In general, Hollywood directors became the arbiters of taste. New stars came to the fore in the thirties: Charles Laughton in *The Private Life of Henry VIII*, Gary Cooper, Katherine Hepburn, Clark Gable, Jean Harlow, Leslie Howard, Vivien Leigh, Greta Garbo and Marlene Dietrich. Perhaps the most typical of them all was Jean Harlow who died after four marriages at the age of twenty-six and whose shiny blond hair and clinging dress provided the working woman of the thirties with her 'model'. (Upper-class people still looked to Paris for their fashionable clothes; working

[1] *Low's Autobiography*, p. 218.

people copied film stars.) 'Harlow' had star personality, but somehow seemed to remain an ordinary girl, and one particularly of her time — never more so than at her funeral which began with 'None But the Lonely Heart' and continued with Nelson Eddy singing 'Ah, Sweet Mystery of Life' and Jeannette MacDonald 'The Indian Love Call'.[1]

10. Jean Harlow

During the thirties cinemas themselves underwent great changes. They had been known as 'palaces' since the beginning of movies, but now they became more obviously places of luxury. Their very names suggested this: the Astoria, Granada, Coliseum, Gaumont, Regal, Rialto, Odeon and Majestic. The idea was to create — often by decorations in an Eastern style — an atmosphere where people could forget present-day realities and see a dream world both around them and on the screen. At the Astoria, Finsbury Park, stars twinkled in the roof and

[1] See article by D. Robinson in *Financial Times*, 2nd July 1965.

looked down on the gateway to a Moorish city which turned out to be the screen. On either side huge columns, minarets and palm trees flanked the audience and in the foyer fish swam in a mosaic fish pond. As the thirties went by cinemas became more functional on the outside, which often looked like a huge concrete block, but inside they still contained many lush fittings. The unemployed of the twenties and thirties received an illusion of comfort inside these 'palaces', for they could not endure the realities that went on in the outside world.

The effect of cinema-going was not always, it was felt, to the good of the public. Many people were particularly worried about the influence on children. When questioned in 1931 Birmingham children said that they had learnt 'to behave yourself or ill will befall you', 'that it is a hard job for the police to catch their culprits' and 'that actresses do not wear enough clothes'.[1] True some films were historical and even educational, but a German researcher analysed 250 films and 'found 87 murders, 52 cases of adultery, 19 seductions, 22 abductions and 43 suicides. Among the principal protagonists were 176 thieves, 25 prostitutes, 35 drunkards, etc.' What, it was wondered, would be the effect of seeing so many people in conflict with society? Many people were predisposed to see the effects as bad, and the Home Office memorandum of 1929 ('Jix', of course, was Home Secretary) gave local authorities, who issued licences for films to be shown in their areas, the power of censorship.

So it is that the film-going public may not see such things as 'indecorous, outrageous and irreverent titles and sub-titles, drunken scenes carried to excess, profuse bleeding, indecorous dancing, improper bathing scenes, scenes in which the King and Officers in uniform are seen in an odious light, disparagement of the institution of marriage, views of dead bodies, scenes laid in disorderly homes and materialization of the conventional figure of Christ.'[2] Other people were more worried that cinema-

---

[1] Birmingham Cinema Enquiry Committee, *Report of Investigations April 1930–May 1931*, p. 15.
[2] Extract from the British Board of Film Censors quoted in J. Laver, op. cit., pp. 73–74.

going was a passive recreation, that the film-fan accepted everything he saw without question and without using thought as to whether actions were right or wrong. In these cases cinema-going was mere escapism and a cheap way to escape at that. 'At a cost of 6*d.* or so a working woman, bored to death by a never-ending round of humdrum household chores, or a factory worker oppressed by the monotony of his work, can be transplanted, as if on a magic carpet, into a completely new world: a world of romance or high adventure.'[1] Rowntree, who wrote these words, was particularly thinking of his home-town, York, where in 1936 seven cinemas provided 7,500 seats for a population of about 89,500 — one seat for every twelve people. 45,000 people attended each week. Three years later there were ten cinemas and weekly attendances were over 50,000, not all different people of course — some went several times a week. Birmingham film fans were even better served. The 1930 directory lists eighty-three cinemas and there were seats for over 115,000. In a survey carried out between April 1930 and May 1931 in Birmingham among children of 8 to 14, it was found that 50 per cent went once a week, 12 per cent twice and 2¼ per cent three or four times. It is not surprising that the Birmingham Film Society's first meeting in 1931 was attended by over 200 people and that the following year Sunday licences were granted.

Sport was the only other field of mass entertainment which could rival such numbers. Sports broadcasts came fifth in popularity in the *Daily Mail's* Gallup poll of BBC listening, and huge crowds of all classes turned up at all professional sporting events, especially football. Everyone played and watched, including the King. In 1923 George V first presented the cup to the winning team of the Cup Final amid a scene of near hysteria. The authorities were unprepared for the 160,000 people who came to the match. The new stadium at Wembley 'had been built to hold 125,000 and the extra 35,000 people overflowed on to the football pitch and held up the game. Nearly three thousand policemen found themselves unable to deal with the situation, for this was before the time of wireless

[1] B. S. Rowntree, *Poverty and Progress* (Longmans, 1941), p. 470.

loudspeakers. When the King arrived in his car the pitch was completely covered with people, and many thousands more were pushing and fighting to get into the stadium. Eventually, a policeman mounted on a grey horse persuaded people to stand back along the touch-lines, and the game started nearly an hour late. A thousand people were injured in the stampede and hundreds were knocked down.'[1]

11. 1923 Cup Final — crowds rush on to the ground at Wembley Stadium

Football in fact was big business. Wembley had been built at a cost of £750,000 and Wolverhampton Football Club gained £110,000 in transfer fees between 1935 and 1939. Even in a city of no exceptional size such as York football crowds in the thirties were usually 4,000 strong for an ordinary match and 12,000 or more for a cup tie. Moreover York ran two pro-

[1] J. Montgomery, op. cit. quoted in J. Laver, op. cit., p. 51.

fessional rugby teams and two professional football teams at the same time (and all could rely on approximately the same support), besides a number of amateur sides. More than 10 per cent of the total population of the town turned out to watch some match or other, and in the North and in parts of Wales professional rugby was often as popular as soccer.

Tennis was the particular sport of the 'bright young things', but all classes who could afford it played to some extent and the Wimbledon tournament attracted thousands of spectators each year. The new centre courts at Wimbledon held 15,000 spectators who watched such tennis stars of the twenties as 'Big Bill' Tilden, Helen Wills and Suzanne Lenglen. Suzanne was often the centre of controversy for she was felt to lack sportsmanship and reliability. On occasions she failed to turn up for matches and in 1926 kept the Queen waiting at Wimbledon. Her tennis outfit was also revolutionary: 'For playing a man's type of game she needed freedom of movement. Off came the suspender belt, and she supported her stockings by means of garters above the knee; off came the petticoat and she wore only a short pleated skirt; off came the long sleeves and she wore a neat short-sleeved vest. Her first appearance at Wimbledon caused much comment, but the practical success of her outfit led to its adoption by others.'[1] Tennis was popular among ordinary people too. In 1936 York had eighteen tennis clubs with total membership of about a thousand, and there were sixty-eight courts in the town. The legacy of the Victorian parks meant that public courts could be provided for hire. At the height of the game's popularity in 1930 the twenty-one tennis courts in York's public parks were let for 15,446 playing hours, despite the fee of 6d. an hour and the cost of buying rackets and balls.

Cricket maintained its hold over its devotees, whether it was at the Oval or on the village green. In 1936 York had no less than sixty-one cricket clubs, but these were clubs for players rather than supporters. No more than a thousand people a week watched cricket. Yet the love of cricket remained a dominant feature of many Englishmen and a defeat in a Test

[1] Lord Aberdare, *The Story of Tennis* (1959) quoted in 43. ibid., p. 43.

Match was treated as a national disaster marked by the headline, 'IS ENGLAND DOOMED?—splashed right across the page and under it the smaller amplifying headlines, and even they were half an inch high:

DEVASTATING ATTACK AT MELBOURNE

HOBBS OUT FIRST BALL: HEARNE 9, WOOLLEY 0

ENGLAND'S APPALLING DEBACLE

CAN HENDREN SAVE US?

In the underground at Sloane Square Station an elderly man in a top-hat and black, velvet-collared overcoat, with an elegant long white moustache, and carrying a rolled up silk umbrella, said fiercely . . . "It all comes of treating it as a game. We don't take things seriously enough in this country, sir, damnation take it all." [1] Cricket hit the headlines most of all in 1933 when, typical for the time, extremists got the upper hand. The practice grew of bowling more quickly and more directly at the batsmen thus causing the 'body-line' controversy. The MCC team that year was much criticized for such action, but it gave an extra excitement to the Test Match and receipts at the gate rocketed! The whole thing was particularly shocking as it was a 'Commonwealth' row and cricket was supposed to show the goodwill and friendship of the Commonwealth countries.

Some towns began to open municipal swimming pools and even allowed mixed bathing, sending up popularity considerably. York had three swimming pools by 1936 which were visited by about 586,000 bathers a year. This popularity was part of the new fashion for sunbathing. Before 1914 it was usual to keep the body covered; after 1918 the fashion was just the opposite: 'Fresh air had won and pushed its victory against the curtain, blind, wrap and flounce so far that it began to pass the Plimsoll Line of Prudery.' [2] New ideas of health taught that sunlight was good especially for undernourished children. Sunbathing was more responsible than swimming for the

[1] A. G. Macdonnell, *England, Their England* (1933) quoted in ibid., p. 35.
[2] G. Heard, *These Hurrying Years* (1934) quoted in ibid., p. 156.

increasing brevity of swim-wear — the more of your body that was exposed to the sunlight the better it was for you.

Another sport, racing, was also very popular. Betting on horses and dogs was one of the main occupations of the men of England — the aristocracy at one end and the unemployed at the other. In 1929, the year of the financial crash, £200 million was spent in this way. Even more significant was the huge amount spent on football pools. In 1936 48,000 pools coupons were posted to families in York — nearly two to every house. In the football season York Post Office sold over 12,000 more postal orders than in the summer, and filling in the coupon had become an obsession. One inhabitant of York admitted, 'A man spends three days in considering next week's football, a day filling in his coupon, and three days in keen anticipation of the following Saturday's results.'

Newspapers and advertising were two more forces which helped to shape the lives of ordinary people in England. Northcliffe with his *Daily Mail* had pointed the way in which the press was going — towards mass circulation and large profits by putting in the papers what people wanted to read, by offering prizes for competitions and free gifts and by selling advertisement space. The price of advertisement space would depend on the number of readers. Circulation stood therefore at the centre of the newspaper industry and the newspaper owners went to absurd lengths to raise their circulation. They 'bought' readers by offering free gifts and so forth. In fact newspaper revenue did not come largely from their sales, but from advertisement revenue. The advertisements were for 'consumer' goods, competing for the spare money of ordinary people. As a result the press tended to keep the public in a buying mood. The *Express* for example went on saying there would be no war even late in 1939. Four papers excelled themselves in the early thirties: the *Daily Mail*, *Daily Express*, *Daily Herald* and *News Chronicle*. Each in 1932 had a circulation of over 1,200,000. In the same year the *Mail* paid £40,000 for the serial rights of Dickens' *Life of Our Saviour* which he had written for his children, and its circulation nearly reached two million. The following year further stunts — the

**SMOOTH,
SILENT POWER
ON
ESSO ETHYL**

Do petrols differ? Esso is the answer. It gives you a new experience in motoring—surging power, delightful acceleration, knockless performance, and a notable saving in your petrol bills. Esso Ethyl is the *only* petrol in which the supercharging Ethyl fluid is blended with the world's most advanced petrol, Esso.

**For lubrication
use Essolube motor oil**

**ESSO
ETHYL**

ANGLO-AMERICAN OIL CO. LTD., WESTMINSTER, S.W.1. *Established* 1888

12. The original 'Tiger in the Tank' (1936)

giving of free sets of encyclopedias and complete Shakespeares for instance — brought the *Herald* and the *Express* to the two million mark. But this wooing of readers was too expensive to continue. Nevertheless Lord Beaverbrook, the owner of the *Express*, kept circulation at this level as well as being distinguished by the fact that his readers came from all sections of society.

Politically the majority of the newspapers with large circulations favoured the Conservative party — 7 out of 10 in 1929. The *Herald* was the most important paper to support the Left, while the extreme point of view, the pro-Russian one, was voiced by the *Daily Worker*. It is difficult to say how papers influenced the mass of the population politically. Probably after the First World War many people would have said they did not believe the newspapers. But it does seem that generally they taught obedience to the government in power and only occasionally pressed any particular point of view, as when Beaverbrook in 1929 tried to promote Empire Free Trade. As far as advertisements were concerned the influence, though unmeasurable, must have been considerable, for papers were aware of their powers of persuasion and sometimes refused advertisements for goods which made over-ambitious or downright untruthful claims. In other ways, with their free gifts, their serials and their film, theatre and book reviews, the press helped to form public taste and the effect of the press was probably greater than that of the cinema.

The large reading public was, of course, one of the results of the growth of education in the inter-war years. Indeed progress would have been even greater if the full provisions of the Fisher Education Act of 1918 had been put into force. Fisher, an Oxford historian and President of the Board of Education, had hoped to create an 'educational ladder' so that everyone who was capable could work his way up from the nursery school to university by means of scholarships and grants. Unfortunately such educational reforms were costly and they were some of the first things to be put aside when the government had to economize on expenditure after the post-war boom. Yet education developed despite the lack of really adequate funds.

Secondary grammar schools in particular increased in size and included more and more scholarship boys and girls. Each L.E.A. (Local Education Authority — county or county borough) had its own methods of giving 'Junior Scholarships' or 'County Minors' and so forth at eleven. Greater interest was also taken in educational research and the twenties and thirties are important for two reports, the Hadow and Spens Reports, which with their ideas of the provision of schools suitable for varying abilities at the secondary stage of education — that is, after the age of eleven — were to have a profound effect on education in the following years, and especially on the 1944 Education Act.

The growth of education was probably one of the reasons why at least a few people disliked or were indifferent to the mass culture of the twenties and thirties just described. For such people there was what may be called 'high' culture: serious literature, music, painting and sculpture for instance. This 'high' culture was very much of its period and yet by its very nature was also set apart from it; it mirrored the desolation and disintegration which resulted from the war but was understood and appreciated by relatively few. This problem of communication between artist and public is present in all spheres of 'modern' art, so that the creative artist has become more and more cut off from the public at large.

The artists least cut off from the public in the inter-war years were writers, even though any experimental work in poetry or prose often received far less than its due from critics and public alike. This was true for instance of David Jones's war novel *In Parenthesis*, written between 1928 and 1937 and consisting of a mixture of free verse and prose, and of the poetry of Edith Sitwell whose free association of words aimed to give an impression of definite objects without describing them, as in *Aubade*:

> Jane, Jane
> Tall as a crane
> The morning light creaks down again
> Comb your cockscomb-ragged hair;
> Jane, Jane, come down the stair.

The war poems of such poets as Sassoon and Wilfred Owen were received much more sympathetically, although (or perhaps because) they debunked the war. However, it was not until 1928 that criticism of the war burst forth like a flood and became popular. By then, ex-soldiers, writers as well as readers, were convinced that the war had been useless: there was no better world to live in and post-war England appeared to be a land of political trickery which prevented progress towards a better state of affairs. These anti-war books included: Sassoon's *Memoirs of Fox-Hunting Man* and *Memoirs of an Infantry Officer*, Ford Madox Ford's *Last Post*, Richard Aldington's *Death of a Hero*, Hemingway's *A Farewell to Arms* and Graves's *Goodbye to All That*.[1] Such books were often frankly autobiographical and it was one of the marks of inter-war authors to 'commit' themselves to their subjects completely and to try to make their readers feel as deeply as they did. In this way writers were breaking free from restraints that had made certain subjects 'unmentionable' before the First World War.

It would certainly have been unacceptable before 1918 to make one's name as an anti-war writer; nor would it have been possible to write and publish successfully political books of an extreme 'left' nature such as those issued by the Left Book Club. But even more typical of the period was the open discussion of sex, and in this sphere the most notable writer was D. H. Lawrence, who wished to free sex from any association with indecency and to help people to live full lives at a time when failure to set the world aright after the war made many people's lives almost unbearable. 'The whole trouble with sex', wrote Lawrence, 'is that we daren't speak of it and think of it naturally. We are not secretly sexual villains. We are not secretly sexually depraved. . . . Our civilization, with its horrible fear and funk and repression and bullying, has almost destroyed the natural flow of common sympathy between men and men, and men and women. And it is this that I want to restore into life. . . . It is the most important thing just now, this gentle

[1] For details of war literature see B. Bergonzi, *Heroes' Twilight* (Constable, 1965).

physical awareness. It keeps us tender and alive at a moment
when the great danger is to go brittle, hard, and in some way
dead.'[1]

Unfortunately, public interest in Lawrence's work all too
often was directed on to those sections of *Lady Chatterley's
Lover* which had to be cut, rather than on the message he was
trying to put over or on his earlier novel, *Sons and Lovers*, and
the later, *The Man Who Died*. Here then is an example of an
artist who failed to communicate with the public in the way he
wished and it was much more true of painters and sculptors
than of writers.

Post-Impressionism had reached England before the outbreak of war and had caused no small scandal. Epstein had
already shocked the public with his statues in the Strand.[2]
Generally speaking, the public went on being shocked with art
throughout the inter-war years. Epstein himself made no
concessions and those who thought that they had come to
terms with the paintings of Picasso were to find his changes of
style from post-impressionism to cubism and every other 'ism'
of modern art mystifying in the extreme. The main influence on
English painting since 1900 was impressionism and the general
public still wished to find in painting and sculpture at least
some exact representation of things they could recognize, while
the artists provided their interpretations of what they saw.

The most popular artists were therefore Richard Sickert,
Wilson Steer and Augustus John because as *The Times* (1935
Jubilee Edition) put it: 'each of them has always remembered
that a picture must be a picture'. In the same way the paintings
of Duncan Grant, Matthew Smith and Paul and John Nash
were reasonably acceptable. On the other hand Henry Moore's
sculptures with their small heads and large bodies were received
with derision, while Barbara Hepworth's smooth, round,
abstract forms were dismissed as worthless. Stanley Spencer's
religious pictures and the gentle romanticism of John Piper's
architectural paintings were more easily understood than the
abstracts of Graham Sutherland and Ben Nicholson, who were

[1] Quoted by W. Bynner, *Journey with Genius* (Nevill, 1953), p. 279.
[2] See John Standen, *The Edwardians*.

nearer in spirit perhaps to the desolation they saw and sensed all around them. Another sign of the time was the presence of a number of women artists, not only Barbara Hepworth, but Vanessa Bell, wife of the artist and critic, Clive Bell, and Laura Knight, a traditional and therefore popular painter.

Some of the music written in the inter-war years was even further cut off from the public than the paintings and sculpture. In Austria Schoenberg and his pupils, Berg and Webern, had broken free from the restrictions of normal key systems and composed on the basis of the twelve notes of a chromatic scale, a scale in which every note was of equal importance. Thus arose twelve tone or atonal compositions in which the 'theme' or 'tone-row' (which was not always easy to distinguish by listening or to remember, but which often looked clear enough on the music paper) was made up of any arrangement in pitch and rhythm of all twelve notes. The disintegration of Europe after the war was thus marked in music by the disintegration of normal composition methods. Just as most people were unready to build a new Europe on new ideals and to find a new function for Europe in the world, in the same way they also failed to understand or appreciate the new developments in music. Schoenberg's and Webern's piano pieces for instance remained outside many people's understanding. Schoenberg's masterwork, his opera, *Moses and Aaron*, was not even staged in England until 1965! Berg fared slightly better, for the underlying lyricism of his Violin Concerto for instance and the sweeping drama of his operas, *Wozzeck* and *Lulu*, made the music more acceptable, though by no means popular.

English composers were less extreme in their modernity than those in central Europe, and were apt to be influenced by Stravinsky, Debussy or Ravel rather than by Berg, Webern or Schoenberg. A folk quality was often present in their work, especially that of Ralph Vaughan Williams, whose *Pastoral Symphony* in many ways belonged to the world of Edwardian England with its peaceful and ordered countryside. But in 1935 came Vaughan Williams' Fourth Symphony in F Minor, a work of unparallelled vigour and strength, whose discordant motto theme was prophetic of the clashes to come in the later thirties in Europe. Another powerful symphony was provided in the same year by William Walton, who had won fame as an *'enfant terrible'* with his entertainment, *Facade* (1923), in which Edith Sitwell's poems were declaimed rhythmically against an instrumental ensemble full of allusions to popular songs and jazz, and with his dramatic choral work, *Belshazzar's Feast*, first performed at the Leeds Festival in 1931. The Leeds Festival Chorus took one look at the score and are said to have damned it as unsingable. Yet sing it they did, and since then it has become both well known and popular. (The survival and increase in number of Music Festivals is, in fact, one of the happiest sides of English musical life between the wars. In 1935 there were nearly 200 music festivals for amateurs, listeners and competitors.)

13. Sir Thomas Beecham

Some English composers were less prone to clashing harmonies and were more readily acceptable to the music lover. John Ireland, Arnold Bax and Arthur Bliss gained some recognition, while Gustav Holst, who was apt to experiment, was known only as a one-work composer — *The Planets*. Two other composers, both of genius in their different ways, were emerging just before the Second World War — Benjamin Britten and Michael Tippett — but before 1939 they were scarcely known at all. One other composer, Frederick Delius, had his name kept before the public through the work of Sir Thomas Beecham.

As in pre-war days, Beecham was responsible for much of the music making of the inter-war years with his promotion of symphony concerts and opera seasons, as well as by the founding of the London Philharmonic Orchestra. He had already spent a fortune on music before 1914. Between 1918 and 1939 he spent — and lost — another, mainly through the expense of running international and British seasons of operas. Artistically all was well, but financially the days of privately-sponsored opera were over. Financial disaster also broke up the British National Opera Company in the twenties. By 1928 they had paid the government £17,000 in entertainment tax but were forced to disband with a deficit of only £5,000. The first Labour Government came to power with good intentions to-wards financing the arts, but, owing to the economic diffi-culties of the country, inten-tions were never transformed into deeds.

The thirties were important for various other developments in the musical life of the country. As *The Times* said in 1935, 'the words "gramophone" and "wireless" point at once to the most significant change in the conduct of musical life during the last 25 years'. The work of the BBC in broadcasting serious music has already been men-tioned, but the BBC also founded the BBC Symphony Orchestra and, under the guid-

14. The Finale of Act IV in the 1934 Glyndebourne production of *The Marriage of Figaro*

ance of Sir Adrian Boult and with a generous allowance of re-hearsal time, a generally higher standard of orchestral perform-ance was reached than was normally possible. Higher standards — or rather a search for perfection — were behind the founda-tion of the Glyndebourne Festival in 1934. In that year John Christie and his singer wife, Audrey Mildmay, began a Mozart opera festival in the theatre attached to their Sussex country home. With the help of conductor Fritz Busch, and producer Carl

D   S.A.T.D.

Ebert, both victims of Nazi persecution in Germany, a degree of perfection was reached never before thought possible. For once the public were ready to pay highly for their seats and to catch the train from Victoria to Lewes in evening dress in the mid-afternoon to attend ensemble performances more perfect than those at Salzburg and Vienna. What is more, despite the views of the pessimists, Glyndebourne was successful, the number of performances increasing each year up to the outbreak of war.

Another success story is that of Sadler's Wells. This was an off-shoot of the work of Lilian Baylis in establishing the Old Vic, where occasional opera and ballet performances were mounted. This grew until opera and ballet were provided with their own theatre, Sadler's Wells, in Islington. There, under the guidance of Lilian Baylis, an opera company was formed, as well as a ballet company under Ninette de Valois, whose presiding genius was eventually to extend over a ballet school and two companies — one resident in London and one touring. But this was in the future. At the time it was an immense struggle for de Valois and her musical director, Constant Lambert. On the one hand there was always the problem of shortage of money; on the other, the need to attract an ever larger audience.

A sizeable and enthusiastic audience was, in fact, one of the great achievements of Sadler's Wells. Even so it was small in comparison with the numbers who went weekly to football matches. There was also, of course, opposition from some die-hards who were against any extension of culture for puritanical reasons or because they disapproved of experimentation and 'high' culture of every kind on principle. In their view it was better that Britain should become, in Sir Thomas Beecham's words, 'the paradise of the low-brow and the bone-head'.

There was no one who was more anti-art than 'Jix' whom we can take as an extreme example of an unfortunately influential attitude. He it was who was responsible for the cuts in *Lady Chatterley's Lover* and for preventing Lawrence's paintings being shown to the public. He backed up the Lord Chamberlain in the censorship of plays. He kept a close watch on all matters which he thought might affect the morals of the country, and, frightened as he was of all progress and change, he saw the free expression of creative artists as a danger to his preconceived ideas. He thus gave the police great powers to stop 'the flood of filth' which was, he feared, ruining the country. Only when the police seized pictures by William Blake as obscene did some people begin to realize the idiocy of such procedures. Nevertheless 'Jix' was among the majority in his hostility to culture. He, like many others, thought that 'the country was healthy while it could be dominated by men with "standards" by which he meant limitations'. Like so many people after the First World War, 'Jix' refused to change with changing conditions. Indeed such people added to the difficulties of society in the inter-war years for, like 'Jix', they were often people of influence. Totally unsympathetic to the time in which they lived, they led the country to social, economic and political disaster.

3

The Economy and Politics after the War

In his autobiography David Low, the cartoonist of the *Evening Standard*, describes how he saw the country's problems in 1919: 'It seemed to me that post-war Britain needed something more than a drastic spring-clean. It needed coordination, economic, financial, industrial and commercial. Everything needed money — mines, railways, industries, agriculture. All required reorganization, regrouping, replanning. A vast capital investment was needed to replace its worn-out industrial plant, and at the same time . . . a wider distribution of wealth or interest to strengthen its social structure, and finally, forward-looking politicians to open the way for energetic businessmen to supply the needs of people devastated or held back in the war. . . . It was a case . . . of building a new future.' Low was certainly right in seeing the importance of the economy in recovering from war. Indeed, Britain's basic problem was *economic* — how the best use could be made of the country's resources; and these resources included labour, skills of mind and body, shipping, money whether invested or at hand to spend, as well as the more obvious imports and exports and natural resources such as coal or iron. It is for this reason that some understanding of economics was urgently needed both at that time and in order to understand those times.

If a plan like Low's had been carried out, then there might well have been 'Homes for Heroes' and 'A Land Fit For Our Boys to Live In', but it would need leaders of immense vision and strength to carry out such a policy. Not only were such leaders lacking but no such policy ever occurred to most of those in charge of the country's economic well-being. In fact the idea of a 'planned economy' just did not exist. Under-standing of economics was still almost entirely at the stage oi observing how the economy worked — how trade, for instance, went in cycles: boom following slump like night following day. Economists had not yet got down to analysing and finding out why trade worked like this and therefore they did not suggest remedies. The old Victorian belief in letting things alone, in the faith that all will come well in the end, still directed most people's actions, so that they were suspicious of specific plans or ideas. In any case the popularity of getting back to normalcy meant that people looked back to before the war rather than forward to the future. This meant that as far as the economy was concerned development and progress on any new lines was almost impossible. It created a straitjacket into which post-war economic conditions would not fit. Yet for the good of the country the economic structure had to be altered, and this is precisely what one government after another failed to do. It was during the economic miseries of this period that slowly and painfully the idea of economic planning was born.[1]

To make matters worse, even individual firms and industries seemed to have lost their enterprise and ability to think ahead. One foreign observer maintained that even before the war the economy needed overhauling, and that after 1918 the need was even greater: 'Old England has been living in a fool's paradise fondly imagining that she could still rely on the spirit and methods of the nineteenth century. Such reforms as have been attempted are insignificant; at any rate up to the War no serious efforts were made to transform coal mining, the metal industry, or textiles — the three bases on which exports and prosperity were founded. England is like a venerable mansion which, though well and solidly built, has for years lacked repairs both in and out.'[2]

The background to the lack of understanding of the economic needs of the country was the ever-present burden and wretched-ness of large-scale unemployment from the ending of the short

---

[1] For the similar situation in the U.S.A., see Hugh Higgins, *Muckrakers to New Deal.*

[2] A. Siegfried, *England's Crisis* (1931) quoted in J. Laver, op. cit., p. 27.

post-war boom in 1920. This continued largely unabated until the outbreak of war in 1939. Indeed, between the wars there was scarcely ever less than one million unemployed. In time this almost seemed to become an accepted condition of life, by the unemployed as well as by the government, and therefore plans to lessen it were never as prominent as they should have been. It was not only industrial workers who were unemployed. Agriculture was also going through a difficult period from 1923 when prices fell. On the whole the worst unemployment was in the old, established industries of Britain, such as cotton and coal, which were mainly in the North and in Wales, so that Britain was as much divided regionally as economically or socially.

15. A queue of unemployed waiting to draw the dole

England had, of course, come out of the 1914–18 war economically weakened. Many ships had been sunk so that the merchant fleet was only a little above half the pre-war strength. This was soon remedied and provided for a while a good source of employment. Another problem was less easy to deal with. England's rich coal resources had been worked unmercifully so that in many mines there were only the more difficult and less rich seams left. Government control remained for a while, together with a government subsidy, but this only hid the problems; it did nothing to solve them. Likewise the Cotton Control Board preserved the nineteenth-century cotton industry almost unchanged at a time when new conditions made it neither appropriately equipped and run nor profitable. Other industries — steel, for instance — which had been encouraged by the war were in an equally difficult position, for they were geared to produce more of certain goods than was necessary in peace time.

All these weaknesses in the economy were symptoms of Britain's economic ills and they all contributed to the unemployment of the period. Moreover, they were aggravated by the country's financial state. Britain had large debts after the war,[1] and her resources of money had been decreased by the sale of many overseas investments. Real recovery was made more difficult, for after the war various debts owed to Britain were repudiated — by Russia after the 1917 Revolution and by certain Latin American States. During the war the National Debt had increased fourteen-fold and the interest on it cost the country a large part of its income from taxation. Although *direct taxes* (such as income tax) were increased after the war, there was no attempt to redistribute wealth and the rich were in most cases still as rich as ever. When the government wished to finance new projects it usually raised loans which increased the amount of money in circulation with the result that the value of money went down and prices went up.

Not that the governments of the interwar years were at all anxious to take on financial burdens, and this seemed common to all parties. The Liberals under Lloyd George were in power from 1919 to 1922 and they had little or nothing to offer the post-war world. They stuck to their traditional policy of free trade and made fulsome promises of what they would do to reconstruct Britain without ever actually doing anything of the sort. Their victory at the polls in 1919 must be put down to the dislike of the other parties and to the personal popularity of Lloyd George, who was felt to have won the war. Lloyd George was the Liberals' last hope but free trade soon proved an inadequate economic doctrine for the post-war world and Lloyd George himself, it has been said, 'was the victim of his own enthusiastic promises of 1918, and of the public wish to

[1] For the international aspect, see P. Bloncourt, *The Embattled Peace.*

find a scapegoat for the unpleasant truth that peace did not automatically bring prosperity'.[1] In any case Lloyd George's government was hardly truly Liberal. It was a coalition which not only included in its government three future Conservative Prime Ministers — Bonar Law, Stanley Baldwin and Winston Churchill (though Churchill was then still a Liberal) — but which also had only 136 Liberals as against 339 Conservatives in Parliament. It is hardly surprising that when the Conservatives came to power under Bonar Law and then Baldwin their economic policy differed but little from that of the previous Liberal-led government.

For the moment, however, Lloyd George had to face the economic problems of the country when the post-war boom burst. He and his colleagues had no long-term plan — indeed they had no plan at all — and they decided to cut expenditure rather than to counter the effects of the depression, when money would be scarce, by spending freely. This was sound old-fashioned thinking, like that of a Victorian housekeeper: if you were living beyond your income, you must economize and do without things. In 1922 the Geddes Economy Committee suggested cuts of over £86 million in government spending — the famous 'Geddes Axe'. Expenditure on the armed forces was to be cut drastically: on the Air Force by £5½ million, the Army by £20 million and the Navy by £21 million. The cost of education was axed by £18 million and war pensions by £3½ million. In the end the government accepted reductions of £64 million in all. In this way they added deflation — the cutting down of money available to spend — to an already depressed economy. What chance had the economy to expand when the government gave this sort of lead to businessmen?

Ignorance of how finance 'worked' was one of the curses of the inter-war years, and it caused much instability, especially when the trend of price rises ended in 1920. Thereafter the fall in prices hit British industries hard, particularly the export industries, which meant that there was much unemployment or 'short-time' as well as demands from employers to workers to accept lower wages. Coal and cotton, which have been called

[1] R. Graves *and* A. Hodge, *The Long Weekend* (Four Square, 1961), p. 69.

'ailing giants', perhaps suffered most of all, and neither was reorganized to any great extent after the war. The situation in these two industries might have been helped by the transfer of workers to new industries such as the motor industry and electrical engineering, but progress was slow as in the twenties conditions were never prosperous enough to help new industries to develop fully. In the difficult years after 1920 the government retreated from any attempt to control the economy. This was true also of the other political parties which from 1922 replaced the Liberals, for, when Lloyd George fell from power in that year, the Liberals as a party fell too. This left the direction of affairs in the hands of the Conservatives and the fast-growing Labour Party, which had already had some success in the election of 1918.[1]

Labour certainly considered itself the party of the future as its election slogans of 1918 showed. They included: 'Land for the Workers', 'A Million Good Homes', 'A Levy on Capital' and 'Nationalization of Railways, Mines, Shipping and Electric Power'. But what did Labour really offer? Despite the brave words, there was no clear-cut or nation-wide Labour policy, for the strength of local pressure was still of great importance and Labour was bedevilled by conflicting local interests and lack of unity. Some unity was gained in 1920 when it refused to affiliate the Communist Party, thus expelling the extremists. In a way this helped to make the Labour Party seem more acceptable and less revolutionary, though a manifesto issued in 1921 made no concessions: 'We of the Labour Party . . . recognize, in the present world catastrophe . . . the culmination and collapse of distinctive industrial civilization which the workers will not seek to reconstruct. . . . The industrial system of capitalist production . . . with the monstrous inequality of circumstances which it produces and the degradation and brutalization, both moral and spiritual, resulting therefrom, may, we hope, indeed have received a death-blow.'[2] Labour party policy-makers talked recklessly about the faults of society in this way, but they were not really

[1] For a parallel discussion see D. Starkings, *British Democracy*.
[2] Graves and Hodge, op. cit., p. 147.

revolutionary, for they wanted to use Parliament to bring about Socialism.

Thus it was to Labour Parliamentary leaders that the initiative passed, such men as Arthur Henderson, Philip Snowden and Ramsay MacDonald. In the election of 1922 nearly $4\frac{1}{4}$ million people voted Labour and the party won 142 seats, becoming thus conclusively the second party in Parliament, but it was not as yet a united party. Labour MPs were uneasily divided between Trade Union representatives and members of the middle class, and its newly-elected leader, Ramsay MacDonald, however charming and sincere a person, was muddle-headed and vague when it came to expressing opinions or acting in a definitely Socialist way. Nevertheless he could dominate his Party as no other Labour leader could, for he was in tune with the age in which he lived, not less than Lloyd George had been during the First World War. MacDonald was, it has been said, 'more avuncular, more eloquent, more uplifting in his confusions than any man of his generation'.[1] He was, moreover, in his moderation responsible for the further acceptance of the Labour Party by the British public at large. He made it look respectable.

16. Ramsay MacDonald

He also did something more: he brought his party to success by forming the first Labour Government, albeit with Liberal support, in 1924. His position as leader was thus assured but he and many of his ministers, under the pressure of ministerial responsibilities, became more moderate than ever. It even appeared that Socialism had been abandoned, and no Labour

[1] N. Angell, *After All* (1951) quoted by J. Laver, op. cit., p. 141.

government was able to deal successfully with the financial and economic crises that occurred when they were in power either in 1924 or between 1929 and 1931. Indeed there seemed to be no distinctive Labour economic policy, for Snowden, Labour's Chancellor of the Exchequer, followed traditional Liberal policies.

Did, then, the Conservatives have any solution to the needs of the country? They certainly had more time than any other party to work out a plan, for, excepting three brief periods, under Lloyd George (1919–22) and under Labour (1924 and 1929–31), the country was more or less continuously under Conservative rule, especially if we count the National Government as Conservative:

Bonar Law	1922–23
Baldwin	1923
Baldwin	1924–29
Baldwin	1931–35
	(MacDonald nominally Prime Minister)
Baldwin	1935–37
N. Chamberlain	1937–39

It is certainly not surprising that the inter-war period has been called the 'Baldwin Age'.

Baldwin himself was to outward appearances an ordinary English gentleman whose family had been successful in business and whose interests were the good of his country and the prosperity of industry. With him as leader the country felt safe and he appeared tolerant and sincere. Behind this straightforwardness there was an astute mind and he was able to make a most unlikely alliance with MacDonald in forming the National Government in 1931 and 1935. It was perhaps Baldwin's power of getting on with people and making other people get on with each other that was his greatest asset, just as common sense was his main stand-by. In contrast to MacDonald's barn-storming, his broadcast speeches were outstandingly successful — he 'went to the microphone and very simply gave a "fireside talk". He was the first political leader to understand the subtle use of the microphone. A week before his broadcast he took the trouble to go to Savoy Hill to obtain advice on how to put it over. . . . Baldwin's quietly spoken plea for a "sane, common-sense Government, not carried away by revolutionary theories or hair-brained schemes", went straight to the heart and home.'[1]

Yet, when it came to actual policy, it was difficult to see what the Conservatives really stood for. One former Conservative Prime Minister admitted as much when he was asked to define the principles of Toryism. He replied: 'I suppose the principles of common sense, to do what seems to be the right thing in a given case.'[2] Despite this negative attitude to policy, the Conservatives were voted into power time and time again, not because of their success in solving the problems of the time, but because of the lack of any more satisfactory alternative. With parties and leaders such as these just described it is hardly surprising that the country was put on the road to economic ruin as soon as economic problems arose.

The day of reckoning came in 1921 when the coal mines were returned to private ownership and the owners decided to reduce wages. The miners came out on strike, at first with the support of the transport and railway workers, who, however, deserted them on 'Black Friday' (15th April 1921). The miners did not give way, but got only poor terms at the end of their struggle — a small government subsidy for a limited period prevented any immediate cut in wages. But the problem was only shelved and the miners pinned their slender hopes on a government enquiry. This Commission under the Liberal leader, Lord Samuel, included William Beveridge, who later wrote the famous report. It made a careful investigation of the whole mining industry and in March 1926 suggested that the coal industry should be completely reorganized to improve conditions of work and to create greater prosperity by managing small pits jointly. For the time being there would have to be a reduction in wages, but the miners would not accept this. They relied on the support of other workers to

---

[1] V. Ogilvie, *Our Times* (1953) quoted by J. Laver, op. cit., p. 61.
[2] Quoted by J. Raymond, 'The Baldwin Age' in *History Today*, September 1960, p. 600.

uphold them if they struck — in fact the nation was on the verge of a dreaded 'General Strike'.

Nor did the mine owners like the report, for they were reluctant to modernize and they wanted a longer working day as well as lower wages. The miners replied in the words of their secretary, A. J. Cook, 'Not a penny off the pay, not a minute on the day.' Whatever history decides on the wisdom of the miners' leaders, few people either then or since have had a good word to say for the owners. One of their political sympathisers called them 'an unprepossessing crowd', and another said more forcefully that 'it would be possible to say without exaggeration that the miners' leaders were the stupidest men in England if we had not had frequent occasion to meet the owners'. The two sides stood immovable, and when the government subsidy came to an end the miners found themselves locked out on 1st May. Many had already ceased to work on 26th April and they expected the fullest support from the TUC, for there was a widespread feeling that since the end of the war far too little had been done to help the ordinary working people.

On 3rd May the General Strike was called, and, besides the miners, transport, railway, heavy industry, gas and electricity workers, builders and printers stopped work. 'Tuesday, May 4th, started', wrote Cook, 'with the workers answering the call. What a wonderful response! What loyalty!! What solidarity!!! From John O'Groats to Land's End the workers answered the call to arms to defend us, to defend the brave miner in his fight for a living wage. . . . It was a wonderful accomplishment that proved conclusively that the Labour Movement has the men and women that are capable in any emergency.'[1] The workers' response was indeed startling — a truly unselfish gesture, for the other workers would not gain any direct benefit from the strike and could ill-afford to exchange their meagre wages for even more meagre strike pay, which in any case came from their own unions' funds. Few had expected that the strike would actually start: 'As I took my ticket home on a bus,' recalls Christopher Isherwood, 'the conductor said: " 'Fraid you'll have to drive this thing yourself, tomorrow, sir." And sure

[1] A. J. Cook, *The Nine Days* (1926) quoted by J. Laver, op. cit., p. 125.

enough next morning, the tremendous upper-middle-class lark began: by lunchtime the Poshocrats were down from Oxford and Cambridge in their hundreds — out for all the fun that was going. . . . Every bus and underground train was a ragtime family party.'[1]

Such a strike was a direct challenge to Parliament, and the strikers and the government both prepared to meet whatever might arise. In this attempt to force a social policy on the government the strikers were unsuccessful. This was not merely because of government action and organization to maintain essential services, but because many of the English, despite the remarkable working-class solidarity in support of the miners, were ready to keep England working — to beat the strike. And how proud many were afterwards that they had beaten the poor and the hungry. Lady Diana Cooper recalls that 'the buses were out, so there were jobs to be done driving workers home to Dalston or Hackney. . . . The wireless for the first time became to us a necessity . . . but, as always in full crisis, the sinews stiffened. . . . The club boys became special constables. My brother was on night duty from nine to six a.m. Some foolhardies were driving buses and trains. I was a free-hand, driving Duff,[2] taking stranded workers home in my car, telephoning Max Beaverbrook for news and being connected to him by Edwina Mountbatten and Jean Norton, who were

17. The unemployed of Jarrow on their march to London, led by a mouth-organ band

[1] C. Isherwood, *Lions and Shadows* (1933) quoted by ibid., pp. 126–127.
[2] Duff Cooper, Secretary for War 1935.

operating the *Daily Express* switchboard. Winston Churchill, in full spate, was bringing out a government news-sheet. Mr. Baldwin was keeping our equilibrium by wise speeches on the radio.'[1] Lady Curzon ran a canteen for night lorry drivers: 'I seemed to spend the whole night frying sausages, and getting my hands burnt by the hot spluttering fat because the sausages were always exploding, until a kind lorry-driver explained in surprise, "Prick them, Miss — prick them".'

18. Undergraduates as volunteer tram-drivers during the General Strike

It was perhaps above all the young who played the most significant part in strike-breaking, particularly university students whose appalling attitude may be gathered from the following reminiscences: 'During my first summer term at Cambridge the normal lawn-tennis programme was upset by the General Strike. However, the greater part of the University rejoiced at the prospect of being able to help defeat the strikers.

[1] D. Cooper, *The Light of Common Day* (Hart-Davis, 1959), pp. 61–62.

I went with a batch of undergraduates to help conduct buses from their depot at Chiswick Park. Unfortunately there were six hundred of us equally keen to conduct the same bus. . . . We went to look for work elsewhere and obtained an excellent job on the railway; but this was too much for the strikers and before we were able to undertake our duties the strike was at an end. After one or two pleasant days of golf, we returned to Cambridge to continue the term.'[1]

All who turned out to work the essential services — the transport of food and supplies for hospitals for instance — started by enjoying themselves but became more and more determined to break the strike. Apart from the working class, most of the public were behind the government in making a success of the emergency arrangements. Even if the strike could not be ended on the playing fields of Eton, at least the Headmaster and fifty of his staff enlisted as Special Constables. Such people probably acted with the best of intentions, yet it can also be said that the General Strike showed 'how bitter the class-hatred from the top, how unscrupulous could be the "gentlemen of England", how crude the prejudices of the middle classes that would never take the trouble to learn the realities of their corporate life until their own selfish individual interests were touched'.[2]

Yet throughout this episode of mild class war there was remarkably little violence. The TUC had always hoped that a compromise could be reached for the miners and they continued to try for this. Such a compromise was arranged in talks with Herbert Samuel and reorganization of the coal industry was to go on at the same time as a reduction in wages. The TUC therefore called off the Strike. This was on the 12th May. But the miners did not accept this solution, for among other things Samuel only spoke for himself and not for what the government would actually do. The miners carried on the Strike futilely and eventually were forced back to work on the owners' terms.

The General Strike appeared to be a total failure. Yet the solidarity of the workers had been shown and there were no further attempts in other industries in the twenties to reduce wages. This is one lesson that the employers learnt, although they learnt it with the self-satisfied smile of victors: 'The Poshocracy had won, as it always did win, in thoroughly gentlemanly manner . . . it was quite prepared magnanimously to pretend that nothing more serious had taken place than, so to speak, a jolly sham fight with pats of butter.'[1]

The government should also have learnt a lesson — the dangers of unemployment in old, unmodernized industries. But unemployment was a question that was never really tackled. Through the Ministry of Labour, in charge of the labour exchanges and unemployment insurance, the government was closely connected with the problem. One of the most important actions of Lloyd George's post-war government was to extend to most manual workers the Insurance Act of 1911 which had been limited to the building, ship-building and engineering trades. By 1921 even workers who had not fully paid in their contributions were allowed to claim benefits and there were extra benefits for wives and families. At this time unemployment had already reached a million, but no one expected that this figure would remain so high. To finance the scheme a special exchequer loan was granted — £30 million in 1921. This can be regarded as the start of the 'dole'. Although it was a burden on the Treasury, it did not seem to the workers to be as humiliating as the poor law benefits had been in the nineteenth century. It made unemployment bearable although it did not solve it.

Even a Labour government could not lessen unemployment. Socialism might have provided an answer but it failed to do so, perhaps, as we have seen, because of its leaders. Instead of taking any positive action, the Labour government of 1924 contented itself with blaming capitalism. The Conservative Government which followed had no remedy and in this way unemployment became accepted; nor was the General Strike taken as a warning. The failure of the coal miners probably discouraged other unions, and the bill forbidding general strikes which was passed in 1927 caused more alarm among the

[1] C. Isherwood, op. cit. quoted by J. Laver, op. cit., p. 127.

Labour movement's leaders than among the workers themselves. Then in 1928 the number of unemployed fell slightly and it seemed that there might be an economic revival. Winston Churchill as Chancellor of the Exchequer[1] was helping certain industries, particularly the railways and agriculture, by relieving them partly from the burden of rates. This kind of subsidy had, of course, to come from the Treasury — the taxpayer was in fact paying to stimulate industry.

But any improvement either in industry or in unemployment was short-lived, for in 1929 came the American financial crash which had repercussions over the rest of the world.[2] It was in late October 1929 that the American boom in speculation came to an end. The resulting fall in prices of shares, the collapse of many companies and banks and the ruin of thousands of individuals affected trade, business and industry throughout America and then all over Europe. It particularly hit shipping, banking and interest on foreign investments, three 'hidden' sources of income on which Britain relied to make up the difference between the value of her exports and the cost of her imports. On the other hand the fall of prices which followed the financial crash favoured Britain, for the same amount of goods could be imported at less cost. In addition, although export industries were hard hit, workers employed in non-export trades found that with wages stable and a fall in prices, they had never been so well off. This brought about one of the contradictions of the period: while there was always a tremendous number of unemployed in the thirties — 2½ million by December 1930 — many people in England prospered more than ever before.[3]

The new Labour Government (formed June 1929) under MacDonald was at a loss to cope with the economic consequences of the crash. Their Chancellor of the Exchequer, Philip Snowden, had no understanding of the need to help industry and relied, as Gladstone might have done, on reducing

[1] See P. Bloncourt, *An Old and a Young Leader*
[2] See *Muckrakers to New Deal* and *Embattled Peace*.
[3] Jarrow had ⅔ of its adult male population unemployed in the thirties, but by 1935 those with jobs were enjoying wages which were only 3 per cent lower than in 1929 while the cost of living was 13 per cent lower.

government expenditure and increasing taxation so that the budget expenditure was equal to income — a *'balanced budget'*. The result was that the country's economic life, already depressed, was given no help or encouragement which could have been provided by the government spending more than usual. But to an 'orthodox' Chancellor like Snowden it was unthinkable to spend more when you were short of money.

In the meantime the conditions of the unemployed deteriorated. A reporter in South Wales in 1931 wrote: 'I gazed out of my hotel bedroom. . . . The sight . . . was one of the most doleful I have ever seen in my life. It consisted chiefly of this: Men — obviously dressed in their Sunday best — standing with their hands in their pockets along the street kerb. Just standing. . . . I knew that if I asked some of them, they would tell me they were "waiting for something to pass by" — a chance to run an errand, or do something to earn a few pence. Others, especially the men over thirty-five (and they are becoming bitter realists now) would answer that they were waiting for the Old Age Pension to come along. These were some of the 15,000 hale, hearty, and capable miners . . . who will probably never go down a mine shaft again in their lives. . . . One man when I asked him what he looked forward to said: "I am just lingering. That's it — lingering." ' None of these miners were incapable of work; there was just no work for them to have and there were thousands like this throughout the country, especially in the North. Jarrow had become an example of 'urban lifelessness; a street which had once been a shopping centre of the town [was deserted]. . . . Between thirty and forty, I think, was the number of shops that had been closed in that little street; their shutters the outward and visible sign of broken homes and hopes'.[1]

This report came from *The Sphere*, an illustrated 'society' journal, where it rubbed shoulders with pictures of such activities as hunt balls. In fact the fate of the unemployed pricked the consciences of some people. When Rowntree, the famous chocolate manufacturer and Quaker social worker,

[1] C. Hamilton, *Modern England* (1938) quoted by J. Laver, op. cit., p. 138.

carried out his survey of York in 1935–36,[1] he could not help but record the pitiful homes and lives of those without work. One family of nine is described thus: 'The man has been unemployed for a considerable time, and receives 32s. Public Assistance. The son, aged 23, is a casual labourer, and earns 35s. The daughter, aged 16, does daily domestic work and earns 7s. 6d. and her food. Together they contribute 24s. The five girls aged 16, 10, 9, 8, and 7, all sleep in one bedroom with their parents, while the sons share a room. There is no sink or water in the house.'[2]

Another workman, aged 29, had 'been out of work for eighteen months and receives 28s. benefit. Wife's father is a builder's labourer. He has been unemployed for two years and receives 17s. benefit. He pays 14s. for his keep. Does not think he will ever get a job now, as the builders want younger men.'[3] Even trained men were not sure to find employment: 'Man aged 31 . . . came out of army six months ago, and has been unable to find a job. Took a six months' course in carpentry before coming out of the army, but feels this was a waste of time and money, as he cannot get a job as a carpenter. Is very keen, and will take on any job he can get. He is receiving 29s. unemployment benefit and has an army reserve of 7s. a week. They rent three rooms in a large house, and have to share the w.c. with four families.'[4]

Rowntree calculated that unemployment caused almost half the worst poverty in York, and he believed that its effects were to be seen not only in poor health and living conditions, but in the demoralizing of the workers: the longer a man remained out of work, the less likely he was to get a job: 'The moral fibre of the unemployed cannot resist either the life they are now leading, or the complacency with which it is accepted. A feeling of slackness pervades the atmosphere; the inspectors . . . often find the . . . unemployed stretched out in bed during the day. For these left-overs, hour follows hour with nothing to do except an occasional visit to the Labour Exchange to see if by chance there is a job to be had. Finally, all effort, aptitude, and

---

[1] Compare this with his earlier survey in J. Standen, *The Edwardians*.
[2] B. S. Rowntree, op. cit., p. 50.   [3] Ibid.   [4] Ibid., p. 51.

energy are benumbed.'[1]

Such men are described by Stephen Spender in one of his poems:

> Moving through the silent crowd
> Who stand behind dull cigarettes,
> These men who idle in the road,
> I have the sense of falling light.
>
> They lounge at corners of the street
> And greet friends with a shrug of shoulder
> And turn their empty pockets out,
> The cynical gestures of the poor.
>
> Now they've no work, like better men
> Who sit at desks and take much pay,
> They sleep long nights and rise at ten,
> To watch the hours that drain away.

Many of the unemployed must certainly have felt that their whole lives were draining away. One man, after six years of unemployment, found himself, his wife and two young children, dependent on his two teenage sons. He was asked what effect unemployment had had on his outlook. He replied: 'It has definitely lessened my interest in politics, because it has led me to believe that politics is a game of bluff, and that these people do not care a brass farthing for the bottom dog.'[2] It seems amazing that communism or at least some revolutionary ideas did not spread among these poor men. They were perhaps too apathetic and ill-nourished to be stirred or perhaps there was no suitable leader to arouse them. Or perhaps they were just too despairing to be deceived by easy remedies.

The politicians of the day did indeed seem incapable of solving the problem of unemployment or even of helping the unemployed adequately or in a suitable way. They had few ideas of their own on such a problem and successive governments knew

---

[1] A. Siegfried, op. cit., quoted by J. Laver, op. cit., p. 139.
[2] H. L. Beales *and* R. S. Lambert, *Memoirs of the Unemployed* (1934) quoted by Ibid., p. 141.

not where to look for advice. They certainly received little help from the financial experts, especially those of the City of London, who so feared the threat of devaluation of the pound that they favoured, like Philip Snowden, a balanced budget by means of a reduction in government spending. And to such people the choice of what to cut was easy — unemployment benefits. Even Snowden was ready to do this, but Labour as a whole shied away from this method. As an alternative tariffs might be introduced to provide extra revenue, but Snowden refused to consider this course of action. The Cabinet could not agree and nine ministers resigned rather than see the unemployed receive smaller benefits. It was out of this situation that the first National Government was formed in August 1931 with MacDonald as Prime Minister and Snowden as Chancellor. Victory had gone to the conformists and Conservatives at the expense of those — the unemployed — who could least bear it.

And so it continued throughout most of the thirties, for there was no real re-thinking of the country's economic policy by any government. The unemployed numbered over a million throughout the thirties while income per head of the population rose steadily, so that, as prices rose only slightly, those in work often appeared quite prosperous. Not so the unemployed and those such as the teachers who had been forced to accept lower salaries during the economic crisis. Their plight remained largely unchanged.

In one sphere at least the economy was brought into line with more recent ideas: this was the gradual change from free trade to protection. This was a path along which many Conservatives had been moving since the late nineteenth century and for which they had been campaigning more actively since Snowden's Budget of 1930 which had removed some duties and which therefore seemed to them a move in the wrong direction.

The whole question of the British Empire and imperial matters was closely connected with trade and protective duties. The Imperial Conference, held amidst the troubled times of 1930, included a serious discussion of protection. Snowden's presence prevented progress, but when Neville Chamberlain, son of Joseph, the main early advocate of protection, was

Chancellor in the Second National Government (MacDonald was still Prime Minister but it was really a Conservative Government) steps were taken to end free trade. In November 1931 duties were imposed to prevent the 'dumping' of manufactured goods in Britain and another act did much the same for fresh fruit, flowers and vegetables.

The following year, 1932, brought a bill which was passed after a perfunctory enquiry into protection by a carefully chosen and sympathetic committee. It enforced a general customs duty of 10 per cent with Empire goods exempted pending the summer conference. Certain goods were placed on a free list — raw materials and most food — and a committee was set up to advise on further duties. The results of the Act were far less extensive and severe than free-traders had imagined, but it was impossible to come to any agreement with the dominions. On the one hand Britain had to protect her own farmers; on the other, the dominions would not encourage trade with Britain by reducing duties. Nevertheless, 1932 marks Britain's departure from free trade to protection.

This change was reaffirmed by subsequent acts. During the next three years no less than seventeen trade agreements were made with other countries by using the bargaining power of duties. In money matters changes came too: the gold standard — the backing of currency by gold — had been abandoned in 1931. The next year, after the pound had been devalued, the Exchange Equalization Fund was set up to 'manage' the currency, to smoothe the problems that would arise from the fluctuations in the value of the pound in international trade. Nothing could have been further from the ideals of free trade, which received its death blow from the failure of the World Economic Conference of 1933 to come to any agreement on the organization of a free world economy.

Such a reversal of economic policy was in some respects revolutionary. It seems that the Conservatives, making up the bulk of the second National Government's supporters, were ready to go to these lengths because they believed that protection would provide an alternative policy to Socialism and at the same time solve the economic ills of Britain. In both these hopes they were ultimately to be disappointed. A policy of protection by itself was hardly likely to solve Britain's economic problems, although the economy did improve gradually in the thirties.

This recovery seems to be more the result of natural improvement than of any government action. Moreover, recovery never came to the worst hit industries and areas. In 1934, by which time the amount of unemployment in the North and Wales and the periodic disturbances and hunger marches had pricked the consciences of the British public, the Special Areas Act embodied the government's one attempt to set up new industries where old ones had decayed, to arrange for the transfer of labour to more prosperous areas — to the car and light engineering industries of the Midlands for instance — and to reclaim and re-plant land. £2 million was provided to finance these plans, but the various government departments failed to co-operate, and improvements in the later thirties in the iron coal, steel and shipbuilding industries were the result of rearmament and not of the Act. By 1937 when the Act was extended it was really too late; unemployment remained until after the outbreak of the Second World War.

Agriculture did not benefit from protection as much as farmers had hoped. From 1920 the prices of farm produce had fallen and in 1921 the government had removed the subsidy on corn as well as guaranteed minimum wages for farm labourers. Ten years later less land was cultivated in England than ever before; there was much unemployment on the land and wages were extremely low; not half of the food consumed in Britain was produced at home. Drastic reorganization was necessary in those places where modernization had not yet taken place and no act of Parliament could really enforce this. Duties could not be used to protect British-grown food if it caused the cost of foreign food to rise: 'stomach' taxes were a matter of practical politics which no political party dared contemplate. Nevertheless agriculture had to be encouraged and saved from unfair foreign competition. Successive governments therefore again fell back on giving subsidies to agriculture — they had reached £40 million in 1936. Such a course of action was largely the result of party politics. All parties wished to gain the agricultural vote.

It therefore seems that the economic situation did improve in the thirties in spite of the government's actions rather than because of them. From 1933 unemployment began to fall and wages to rise. In 1935 Chamberlain claimed that the country had recovered 80 per cent of its prosperity, but vast numbers still remained out of work and many had been embittered by the cuts in benefit and the use of the 'means test' (to see if the unemployed had any other source of income besides the benefit) made in the economies of 1931. Matters had been improved by the Unemployment Act of 1934. Although this was so unpopular at first that there were demonstrations and hunger marches, eventually it made the change from 'benefit' to 'assistance' under the control of the Unemployment Assistance Board.

No plan was ever worked out to try to end unemployment. Politicians still saw the problem as one whose evils should be mitigated and not as one whose causes should be diagnosed and then cured. Not even the leading economists of the day came to grips with the problem. They were all too ready to suggest that measures should be taken to help revive industries although very often these very industries were unsuitable and unable to be saved, however much encouragement they received from the government. Instead the whole industrial structure of the country needed overhauling. Britain's industries were trying to play the part they had taken in the nineteenth century without considering the altered circumstances of the twentieth-century world. This was, of course, a problem which all countries were having to face in the years after the First World War. All countries suffered from the slumps, unemployment and financial disasters of the twenties and thirties to some extent. Until they could find a way for development suitable to the twentieth century, it would appear that they were destined to fail.

The failure of British industry and economic policy in the years between the two world wars is not always sufficiently apparent. At the time the problems of the depression following the financial crash of 1929 were so overwhelming that the fact that there was any recovery at all seemed remarkable. Moreover, the relative prosperity of many people in some areas in England in the thirties made recovery look more real than it actually was. The policy of rearmament in the later thirties did much to help the worst hit industries of the north, though this could hardly be seen as a permanent means of employment. As it was, the failure to adapt Britain's economy to the twentieth century was covered up by the onslaught of the Second World War which brought with it full employment and a planned economy such as the country had needed since peace in 1918. But the fact that the economic problems had not been solved in the inter-war years meant that they remained to be solved after the Second World War. Some of these problems — those concerned with coal and the railways for instance — still need to be solved today.

4

Life in the Thirties

It is always difficult in studying history to see society in a proper perspective — to see it as a whole. It is particularly difficult in studying the thirties when everything was overshadowed by economic failures and the overwhelming misery of unemployment. Yet there was another side to life even in those dismal days, for the standards of living among the middle classes and among those workers who still had jobs were rising fairly steadily.

This new-found prosperity was to some extent confined to the south-east corner of the British Isles and was closely connected with new techniques and products. The electrical and radio industries, for instance, grew quickly for there was a great demand for electrical gadgets of every kind and for the newest models in wireless sets. Car production too grew apace and provided employment for technicians and for workers in all the allied trades. The development of a new material, rayon, gave some boost to the hard-hit fabric industries of Britain, and plastics of all kinds were just coming on the market. People could afford to buy such products if they were in a safe job, because prices were falling and because with world trade diminishing there was less competition from foreign-produced goods.

For these people in 'safe' jobs — for such as bank clerks, insurance agents, cinema operators, garage proprietors and mechanics and electrical engineers — life in the thirties was not at all unpleasant. In fact some people can look back on the thirties as a time of plenty. Middle class families could have their own cars and get about more easily. Ford and other large car manufacturers produced small cars which such people could afford — the 'Ford 8', 'Morris 8' and the 'Austin 7' or 'Baby Austin'. This development had begun before 1930, and

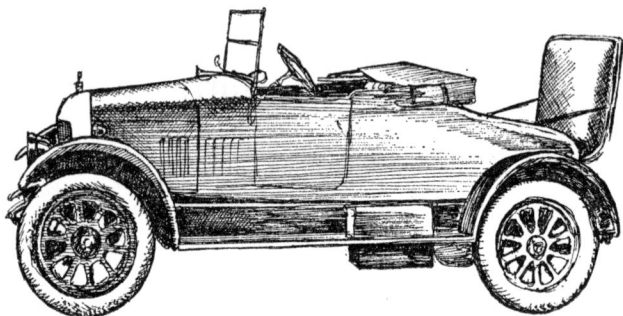

19. Two-seater Morris Cowley with double dickey

the following figures show how motor vehicles ousted horse-drawn ones from the road:

Date	Private Cars	Motor Cycles	Commercial Goods Vehicles	Horse Drawn Vehicles
1922	314,769	377,943	150,995	232,865
1930	1,042,258	698,878	334,237	52,414

By 1939 private cars alone numbered two million.

Cars helped to make it possible to live further away from town centres and thus another sign of prosperity was the growth

20. New houses near Bromley in Kent, 1925

of suburbs, for the thirties was a great age of house-building —
great, that is, in number if not in quality. Between 1934 and
1939 three million houses were built, mainly cheap little villas,
rather like boxes by the side of bypasses and roads leading
out of towns. They usually had patches of garden, back and

21. Design for a drawing-room in 1933

front, and sometimes they were designed in an unattractive
(and quite unnecessary) mock-Tudor style, rejoicing in such
names as '*Mon repos*' and '*Mon abri*', but inside they still
consisted of three bedrooms, a bathroom, a lounge, a dining-
room, and a little 'labour-saving' kitchen. Such houses cost about
£700 to put up and, although they were often poorly built, they
were much in demand as status symbols. People who bought
them felt that they were better housed than those who remained
in older houses. For a greater outlay of money much larger
and more opulent houses could be built on the outskirts of a

town — fairly faithful 'Tudor' houses with *real* rotting wooden beams and 'hand-made', artistic bricks and tiles. These houses were for the stockbrokers and business men who moved out of towns, for instance to Surrey and Kent. You could investigate the spread of this kind of building in your own area from Ordnance Survey Maps.

Inside these houses there were also signs of prosperity and of the new industries that were helping to make Britain prosperous again. The wireless, of course, was almost universal. Television did not come till 1936 and it was only found in very few homes before the Second World War; but most middle-class families had electricity, and labour-saving devices such as vacuum cleaners, electric irons and cookers (often bought on hire-purchase) were becoming much more common. Meals were also easier to prepare by using 'prepared' foods such as packets of breakfast cereals instead of home-made porridge, and tinned and processed foods of all kinds.[1]

All these goods are what we call *consumer goods,* and it became more and more necessary for industry to capture the markets for such goods in order to make a profit. Advertising therefore increased to become an industry in its own right, an industry that tried to create wants and to sway buyers. Slogans used in advertising became well-known and were repeated even if they were not strictly true. Hire-purchase also helped to boost sales as did commercial travellers for such goods as vacuum cleaners. All this made the middle class more and more gadget-conscious, and interest was further roused by *The Ideal Home Exhibition* run by the *Daily Mail,* for newspapers, as we have seen, were now depending on advertising just there kinds of consumer goods for their profits.

Nevertheless, whatever the motives of industrialists and advertisers, the buying of consumer foods in large quantities in the thirties indicated that at least one section of the community was fairly prosperous. But this very prosperity brought its problems. Advertising itself could have ill effects and be misleading. We have already seen that the new houses erected

[1] See Ann McKenzie, *The Hungry World.*

were often ill-designed and some were jerry-built, while the determination to get away from towns meant that cities began to sprawl out along the main roads.

22. Design for the 1931 *Daily Mail* Ideal Home Exhibition

On the roads themselves prosperity had introduced a killer — traffic. In 1929 there were 6,896 road deaths — more than in 1959. The thirties had to work out a new technique of traffic control. At first there were not even driving tests until voluntary ones were introduced, and there was no adequate police control or even road space. Driving licences were introduced not at first to control, but to tax, because roads were so inadequate and needed vast sums of money spent on them. Traffic lights, pedestrian crossings and 'Belisha' beacons (introduced by Hore-Belisha when he was Minister of Transport, 1934–37) did not come until later. Indeed one wonders if Britain has ever really tackled the problem of traffic.

But these problems of prosperity for the lucky few in the thirties were overshadowed by the far greater problem of the poor. That the poor remained such a problem was, in some ways, surprising. It was now generally accepted that the state should try to help the less well-off members of society, especially at certain periods of life and during certain conditions — old age, illness, and unemployment, for instance. During the period between the wars Parliament passed laws to deal with these problems. The Welfare State — a term not used until 1947 — was gradually being created. Here is a list of some of the landmarks:

1919 Housing and Town Planning Act including a plan for Local Authorities to subsidize council house rents.

1919 Non-contributory pensions at 70 raised to 10s.

1920 Unemployment Insurance Act extended that of 1911 so that nearly all workers had 15s. a week (12s. for a woman) for 15 weeks after 12 contributions.

1925 Widows, orphans and old age contributory pension scheme gave 10s. a week to insured workers at 65, 10s. to widows and 7s. 6d. for an orphan child.

1927 Unemployment Insurance Act reduced benefits and tightened up the system.

1929 Local Government Act abolished Poor Law Unions and Boards of Guardians so that poor relief was now organized by County Councils.

1931 Unemployment Act set up the Unemployment Assistance Board which was responsible for all able-bodied unemployed. It widened the number eligible for relief, and included boys of 14 to 16. (Agricultural workers were not included in an unemployment insurance scheme until 1936 and domestic servants not until 1938.)

1935 Housing Act forced local authorities to plan to abolish slums and overcrowding. (By 1939 over a million people had been re-housed, for the 1935 Act was followed up by other measures and was fairly successful despite the

reduction in 1938 of the subsidy given for slum clearance.)
1936 Health Insurance now covered over 19 million people
(about half the population over 14) but wives and mothers
were unprovided for, except when child-bearing, and
only children of school age had the chance of medical
inspection.

These are only a few of the Acts which helped to create a
system of welfare and the gaps are obvious and many — the
working-class wives and mothers in particular and many of the
old. But on the whole British people in the thirties were quite
proud of the social legislation that had been passed, especially
those who were comfortably off. They were apt to think that
poverty only existed in the 'special' or distressed areas of the
North and Wales and that unemployment could be cured. They
saw, in this case with some truth, that the poor of their day were
not so poor as the Edwardian poor, not even the unemployed
man keeping his family on the dole. Yet the number of poor
was considerable and to see the extent and depth of this poverty
that still existed despite the government's efforts, we can turn
to the research of Seebohm Rowntree.

From 1935 to 1936 Rowntree, thirty-six years after his
original survey of York, made a second survey of the town, a
survey which included 16,362 families — almost all of the
working class of the town. His aim was clearly stated: 'I
determined to repeat the investigation made in 1899 and to find
out what changes had occurred in the living conditions of the
workers during the thirty-six years which had elapsed since my
previous investigation was made. I felt that the considerable
labour which this would involve would be worth while because
that period had been one during which more far-reaching steps
had been taken to raise the standard of life of the workers than
during any previous period of similar length.'[1]

As before Rowntree fixed a poverty line, basing his calcula-
tions for a family of five (mother, father and three children) on
1936 prices. After rent had been paid, such a family would need
43s. 6d. per week. This sum was made up of the following items:

[1] B. S. Rowntree, op. cit., p. v.

	s.	d.	
Food	20	6	(based on the necessary vitamins to maintain health)
Clothing	8	0	
Fuel and light	4	4	
Household sundries	1	8	
Personal sundries	9	0[1]	

But again as before in order to gain the maximum benefit from this amount of money the housewife would have to consider every article bought extremely carefully. The food would have to be the most nutritious at that price. There could never be any expenditure on goods which were not essential, nor any waste of any kind. Few families had the inclination let alone the knowledge to live such puritanical lives. Unwise spending and wastefulness therefore put many people below this poverty line — many more than Rowntree calculated — for one glass of beer or twenty cigarettes was all that was needed to tip the balance.

No one could say that Rowntree's standard was too lenient. Yet he found that 31·1 per cent of the working class, or 17·7 per cent of the total population, of York were living below this basic standard. Moreover, if 10s. leeway were given to provide for occasional non-essential expenditure or wastefulness, thus taking 53s. 6d. as the necessary minimum, a further 18·9 per cent of the working class (or 10·8 per cent of the whole population) must be added to those who were living in poverty. The total on this reckoning would be 50 per cent of the working class or 28·5 per cent of the total population.

Rowntree drew from his report a graphic picture of what life for the poor was like in his chapter 'Life Below the Minimum'. The examples tell their own story:

2 bedrooms, kitchen and scullery. Rent 6s. 6d. Unemployed man aged 48, wife 39 and 10 children aged 18, 17, 15, 13, 12, 9, 8, 7, 4 and 1 month. Son, aged 18, earns 25s. per week. The one aged 17 earns 17s. The girl, aged 15, earns 14s. Together they contribute 44s. The father receives 34s. Public Assis-

[1] Ibid., p. 28.

tance. The house is very dirty and much overcrowded. The husband has not worked for years and says he is much better off on the dole. This family has been helped in every conceivable way, and the husband has been known to sell things which have been given for his family. One bedroom has two beds, but the other is only large enough for one. Two children have died. The wife has been twice in a sanatorium suffering from tuberculosis.

Total family income (including the value of the free milk at school), 94s. 6d. Available income (i.e. after the rent has been paid) 81s. 6d. Deficiency 3s. per head.[1]

Here we can see that the problem is one of unemployment and illness aggravated by a large number of children. This was not always the case; unemployment and illness were quite sufficient to condemn a family to poverty:

2 bedrooms and kitchen. Rent 5s. 7d. House scheduled for demolition. Widower aged 37, and 2 children aged 15 and 10. Man is an unemployed general labourer. Has been unemployed for seven years, and receives 19s. benefit. Previously he was a carter but had to give this up as he has a weak heart. The girl aged 15 works in a factory and earns 15s. 6d. She contributes 13s. There are bugs in the woodwork in the bedroom.

Total income, 34s. 6d. Available income 32s. Deficiency 3s. 2d. per head.[2]

Another cause of poverty is seen in the following example:

1 bedroom, 1 attic and kitchen. Rent 6s. Man aged 23, and wife 18. An addition to the family is expected. The man is employed at a shop, and is paid 30s. a week. The house is in a bad state. The attic cannot be used. They share the yard and a w.c. with another family.

Total family income, 30s. Deficiency, 4s. per head.[3]

Here an inadequate income seems to be the sole cause.

Rowntree himself analysed the causes of poverty in the

---

[1] Ibid., p. 49.   [2] Ibid., p. 51.   [3] Ibid., p. 57.

section of the working class living below the minimum. His findings were as follows:

Out of 17,815 people who lived in poverty
32·8% did so because of inadequate wages of chief wage earner
28·6% did so because of unemployment of chief wage earner
14·7% ,, ,, ,, ,, old age
9·7% ,, ,, ,, ,, inadequate wages of other workers
7·8% ,, ,, ,, ,, death of husband
4·1% ,, ,, ,, ,, illness
2·5% ,, ,, ,, ,, other reasons

75 per cent of this poverty could therefore be removed if wages were increased, if reasonably paid employment could be found

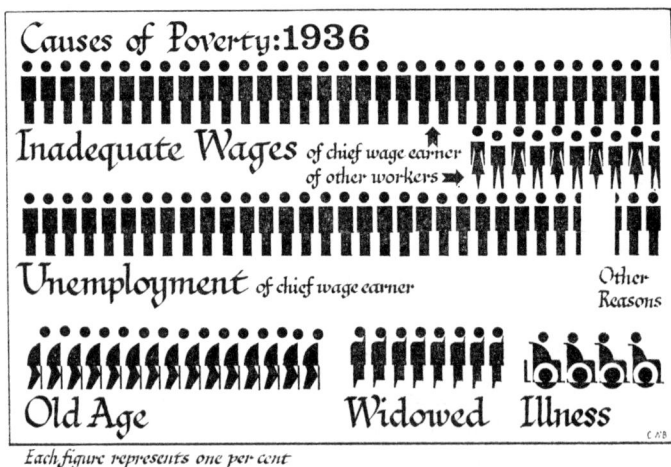

Each figure represents one per cent

Fig. 23.

and if adequate old age pensions were provided. One begins to wonder whether perhaps York was particularly depressed at this time, but Rowntree maintained that the two main industries of York, the railways and chocolate making, which between them employed about 18,000 people, provided wages that were good in comparison with other industries in Britain. He concluded that 'from the standpoint of the earnings of the workers, York holds a position not far from the median (or average), among the towns of Great Britain. If on the one hand there is no important industry employing a large number of highly skilled and highly paid workers, on the other hand there are no large industries (though unfortunately there are isolated small businesses) where wages are exceptionally low'.[1]

Two conclusions may be drawn. Firstly, workers' wages over the whole country would therefore seem to be below a satisfactory living standard, and secondly, we must ask ourselves a further question: what made the wages inadequate? One reason was undoubtedly the nature of the work — such people as shop assistants, builders' labourers and transport workers were almost always paid only small wages, and there was often little chance of getting promotion in such jobs. These workers often experienced a cycle of poverty. When they first worked they would be fairly well off, but would experience a fall in the standard of living when they married, unless their wife remained at work. Poverty almost always followed or increased when children were born, for a wage that kept one person well and a married couple without want was inadequate for a family. In fact unless a wage were paid that would maintain a family of five (an average family) above the minimum, wages would remain inadequate. Until the children went out to work or until the wife could go back to work, such families would remain in poverty. Thus at the very time when expenses were greatest and when the needs of the mother and children were at their peak, the family would be living in its greatest need.

The circumstances of such a family described as follows:

2 bedrooms, sitting-room and kitchen. Rent 6s. 9d. Man aged 30, wife 32 and 3 children aged 6, 4 and 11 months. The man is a baker's labourer, and receives 38s. a week. The w.c. is shared with another family. House is very unhealthy.

[1] Ibid., p. 10.

Previously lived in a Council house, but had to give this up because the rent was too high.

Total family income, 38s. Deficiency, 2s. 6d. per head.[1]

Here we have a family whose standard of living had been reduced when their children were born, and we can also see that plans for providing Council houses although commendable were not always successful in helping those most in need of better accommodation.

Closely connected with living conditions was ill-health as a cause as well as a symptom of poverty. Illness, moreover, had little chance of proper treatment when there was poverty and thus illness was often made worse. In York tuberculosis accounted for a tenth of the illness, and was only exceeded by war injuries. Yet the assistance given from friendly societies, Health Insurance and the Public Assistance Committee was completely inadequate. The ill who were in poverty could thus look forward to nothing more than old age in even worse health and in greater poverty.

Whatever the reason for poverty, all poor suffered from lack of suitable food. With their very limited means great knowledge would have been necessary to obtain the most nutritious food. Rowntree found that all families living below his minimum were underfed even when they spent enough actual money on food. This state of affairs existed despite the increased knowledge of nutrition and was all the more noticeable because the better off sections of society fed well and had greatly improved their diet since pre-war days. As far as the poor were concerned there had been little improvement in their diet since Rowntree's first report on poverty. This was particularly true of the unemployed living on the dole when they had children, for the additional grants given by the Assistance Board for children were quite inadequate. It is instructive to study such a family in detail.[2]

A man, wife and 4 children had to exist on 36s. a week unemployment benefit, and, after other necessities had been bought, an average of 16s. 10d. was left for buying food. This provided such meals as the following:

[1] Ibid., p. 58.   [2] Ibid., pp. 188–189.

	Breakfast	Dinner	Tea	Supper
Fri.	Bread, dripping, tea	Cod (2 lbs), potatoes, bread, butter, tea	Bread, butter, tomatoes, jam, tea	None
Sat.	Bacon ½ lb, bread, dripping, tea	Minced meat (¼ lb), potatoes, bread, butter, tea	Bread, butter, potted meat, tea	Cocoa

For the money spent the housewife got good value and organized a varied menu, but the diet showed a deficiency in protein (51·2 per cent) and calories (27·7 per cent), and the expenditure was grossly inadequate on milk for a family with three young children — 7½ pints was the most bought in any week. But knowledge of what to buy was not enough. To feed this family adequately, at least 24s. 3½d. would be needed and there was nearly 8s. less than this sum available. Rowntree admitted that this was one of the best managed families and his findings led him to believe that the only way to obtain adequate nourishment was to increase the income of all families below the minimum or to lower the cost of food.

Diet, of course, had far-reaching effects on the lives of the poor. It affected their general health which in turn had repercussions on their ability to work. In the end it also affected their span of life. The figures giving the death-rate for children under one year of age per 1,000 births tell their own story: for York as a whole the rate was 56·1 per 1,000; for those living below the minimum 77·7 — nearly half as many again. The overall death-rate showed the same tendency in being over a third as high for the poorest section of the community than for the highest grade of the working class.

Nevertheless Rowntree was able to point out many improvements when comparing his surveys of 1899 and 1935–36. In 1936 poor people were healthier; they had more food; children were taller and heavier; fewer children died in infancy; more people lived to old age; housing conditions had improved; and there was much less abject poverty. When the 1899 standard of primary poverty was applied to the poor in 1936, it was found that, whereas in 1899 15·46 per cent of the working class (9·91 per cent of the total population of York) were living in primary poverty, in 1936 the comparative figures were 6·8 per cent and 3·9 per cent: an improvement, even if the governments of inter-war years had not yet done nearly enough to help the really poor.

This problem even affected the somewhat insensitive consciences of the time. Most kindly people had at least a vague feeling that something ought to be done about it, only what? Very few people ever decided what would be best. To make matters worse, so many of the thin, tired men who hung about the streets had service medals pinned to their threadbare clothes. What had happened to the comradeship of the trenches, and the hopes of a 'Land Fit for Heroes'? In 1933 J. B. Priestley went to his old battalion's reunion in Bradford: 'Several of us had arranged with the secretary to see that original members of the battalion to whom the price of the dinner was prohibitive were provided with free tickets. But this . . . had not worked very well. . . . They were so poor, these fellows, that they said they could not attend the dinner, even if provided with free clothes. . . . They ought to have known that they would have been welcome in the sorriest rags; but their pride would not allow them to come. . . . They were with us . . . in that early battalion of Kitchener's New Army . . . and they stood in the mud and water, scrambled through the broken strands of barbed wire . . . and came back as official heroes . . .; and now, in 1933, they could not even join us in a tavern because they had not even decent coats to their backs. We could drink to the tragedy of the dead; but we could only stare at one another, in pitiful embarrassment, over this tragi-comedy of the living, who had fought for a world that did not want them, who had come back to exchange their uniform for rags! And who shall restore to them the years that the locust hath eaten?'[1]

Not all the poor were ex-soldiers of the First World War, but their condition was just as pitiable. The majority were under-nourished; many were ill-housed; not a few were in a state of chronic ill-health; nearly half were unemployed and lived on the dole or eked out their lives on some kind of public assistance.

[1] Quoted by J. Raymond, op. cit., p. 606.

'The existence of this class', wrote Rowntree, 'constitutes a challenge to the community to find ways by which poverty, such as we have been considering, shall become a thing of the past.'[1] Unfortunately, this challenge was never met in the inter-war years.

[1] B. S. Rowntree, op. cit., p. 100.

5

Public Opinion after the War

Since the social and economic situation of the inter-war years failed to provide 'homes fit for heroes' or even a basic minimum of security for many, it might be asked whether the politicians of the day, who were responsible for social and economic policy, really understood these problems. And as one looks closely at the political scene it becomes apparent that the politicians were not far different from the politicians of the pre-war period. The world had changed but they had remained. They remained, moreover, as aliens in a strange, new and, to them, unwelcome world. To those Englishmen who had hoped for a new world after the war the lack of policy looked like political trickery; to those few politicians who knew the need for change, the lack of policy looked like imbecility; to the majority of politicians change was more often than not a mere impossibility. These three factors — trickery, imbecility and impossibility — made the politics of the inter-war years overwhelmingly disappointing.

There was a greater number of people who took an active interest in politics than previously. More people than ever before had the vote, especially after 1918 when women were enfranchised if they were over thirty and after 1929 when women were given the vote on the same terms as men. There was some outcry against giving political power to women in 1919 — many conservative men felt that it was wrong to give a voice in politics to the 'flappers', as the young women of the twenties were known. Women only became a force in politics gradually. At first it may be presumed that most of them voted for the party supported by their husbands or fathers.

In time the growth of education, and especially of girls' secondary education and of opportunities for higher education for young women, meant that this new half of the electorate had to be wooed at elections — not only for their own vote but for the influence they might bring to bear on their husbands and children. One aristocratic canvasser was well aware of this problem when she electioneered for her husband: 'Canvassing

23. Lady Diana Cooper in door-to-door political canvassing

at all times I find miserably disagreeable — the knock on the door and the housewife's unpredictable mood, influenced by whether she has the dinner or high tea in the making, is wringing linen or having a nap. Her head is poked out of the door, and if she recognizes the Party she favours she will open it wider, dry hands, and say: "Come forward." She may be ready to talk about politics or wages, or she may say: "We have always voted Blue and always shall." She may ask questions showing an unmade-up mind or she may . . . take refuge behind the secrecy of the ballot. I marvelled when they did not bang the door in our silly, smirking, out-to-please faces.'[1]

It was, of course, not only women who became aware of politics through the growth of education. Many men were able to take a more intelligent interest, especially when hopes of a 'new' England failed to materialize after the war. Not that greater intelligence meant a change of tactics on the part of prospective MPs. Lady Curzon tried to help her son in the East End in 1923: 'I took a furnished house in East Ham — a nice, funny little house full of aspidistras — and I took my French maid with me, and we had Hubert's batman, and I had my Rolls-Royce and the chauffeur. We lived on hampers of food from Fortnum and Mason's, and I canvassed while Hubert was touring the constituency making speeches.'[2] It is hardly surprising that this kind of help was not successful.

Such behaviour did not appeal to the East End electorate, but a different approach was tried at Acton in the following election campaign: 'We imported a bevy of beautiful young women to work and canvass in the constituency, and some of the results were quite amusing. I shall never forget a man who shouted, "Make that hussy go away from my door!" — pointing to lovely Diana Cooper standing, canvass-card in hand, on his doorstep.'[3] At this election, whatever the reason, Hubert was successful. The comments of those who took part hardly help us to feel that politicians realized that they were dealing with a more knowledgeable public than ever before — men who had had at least some schooling and who had gained an 'apprenticeship' in politics through responsible work in their local unions and who went on educating themselves through evening classes and the activities of the W.E.A.[4]

In one respect the inter-war years were a period when there were more intelligent people who wanted to take part in active politics than before or, perhaps, since, and this made it a great age for the intellectuals in politics — those who tried to think

[1] D. Cooper, op. cit., p. 41.
[2] The Marchioness of Curzon, *Reminiscences* (Hutchinson, 1955), p. 241.
[3] Ibid.   [4] The Workers' Educational Association.

clearly about the problems of government and to act according to a properly worked out theory. As the politicians in parliament in the early twenties gradually seemed to waste their opportunities and to make a mockery of all that the soldiers of the First World War had fought for, these young intellectuals jumped on the first 'cause' that came along so that they could lampoon the bungling government. It took some time for the intellectuals to come to the forefront, but by the late twenties and especially after the economic crash of 1929, they played a significant part in the political life of the nation. All sides had their intellectual supporters, but most young intellectuals supported the Left, as Labour came to be called, for it was the Left which felt that the post-war governments of the twenties had betrayed them. They even felt they had been betrayed by the Labour Party's own leader, Ramsay MacDonald, who appeared so moderate that he was scarcely distinguishable from a Liberal or a moderate Conservative. Moreover, from August 1931, when he formed the first National Government and the majority of his party refused to follow him, he appeared to be leading a Conservative Government rather than a coalition.

It was such forces as these that brought forth the British intellectuals of the Left: 'Between 1928 and 1933 a change occurred in their outlook. . . . A new seriousness came to the fore. . . . Increasing attention was given to politics. Whereas sex and aesthetics had been the major topics of conversation, now everybody began to talk politics. As time passed the politics of the intellectual moved leftward to socialism and communism.'[1] Labour had always had a small minority of intellectuals in the members of the Fabian Society, such people as Geoge Bernard Shaw and Sidney and Beatrice Webb. But now the intellectuals who supported the Left were extremists and not at all like the usually moderate Fabians. Previously, extremists had been members of the working class or union leaders. The new extremists seemed at first much more dangerous. For one thing they included a number of influential writers — W. H. Auden, Rex Warner, Christopher Isherwood,

[1] N. Wood, *Communism and British Intellectuals* (1959) quoted by J. Laver, op. cit., pp. 168–169.

Cecil Day Lewis and Stephen Spender for instance — who could popularize their views in books, pamphlets and poems. Often they were sympathetic to Marxism, admired Soviet Russia and sometimes became members of the Communist Party.

To such people joining the Communists (or The Party) was the logical conclusion: 'Paradoxical as it may seem Communism has . . . a particular appeal to people brought up in British public schools and universities, especially with a classical and Christian education.'[1] This is explained by the poet Cecil Day Lewis: 'Nearly all my friends who during this period became active in Left Wing movements, or at least sympathetic to Left Wing ideas, had had the same kind of upbringing. Rex Warner, MacNeice and myself were sons of clergymen; Auden had a devout Anglo-Catholic mother; Spender came from an "old-fashioned Liberal" family. We had all been to public schools, with their traditions both of authoritarianism and of service to the community. We had all, I think, lapsed from the Christian faith, and tended to despair of Liberalism as an ineffective instrument for dealing with the problems of our day. . . . I daily felt the need of a faith which had the authority, the logic, the cut-and-driedness of the Roman church. . . . Marxism appeared to fill the bill. . . . I had hope: no one who did not go through this political experience during the thirties can quite realize how much hope there was in the air then, how radiant for some of us was the illusion that men could, under Communism, put the world to rights.'[2]

Before they could do this it was, of course, necessary for their views to be spread. It was here that the publisher Victor Gollancz played an important part. In 1935 he started the Left Book Club, which made available to members (who soon numbered 50,000) two books every month at a special cheap rate. Gollancz was helped in the choice of books by two extreme Left-wing writers, John Strachey and Harold Laski, so that the Club in fact produced a stream of Socialist and Communist propaganda. Members of the Club had their views

[1] C. Cockburn, *Crossing the Line* (1958) quoted by ibid., pp. 170–171.
[2] C. Day Lewis, *The Buried Day* (1960) quoted by ibid., p. 171.

further coloured by articles in *The Left Book Club News*. So influential did the Club become that one bookshop owner put this in his window:

> 'Forced to make the choice themselves,
> Our rude forefathers loaded shelves
> With Tennyson and Walter Scott
> And Meredith and Lord Knows What!
> But we don't have to hum and ha,
> Nous avons changé tout cela —
> Our books are chosen for us — thanks
> To Strachey, Laski and Gollancz!'[1]

Indeed the influence of the Club on what people thought can scarcely be overestimated. The books were read by many others besides left sympathisers and they were especially popular among undergraduates. It became the 'done thing' for a student to have decided political views, preferably of a leftish nature. The Oxford Union went as far as voting by a majority that 'in Socialism lies the only solution to the problems facing this country'. The young really did believe in salvation from the Left. Some were doomed to disappointment when they realized that the Labour Party was ineffective in office. Others who joined the Communist Party came to realize that in practice communism prevented the freedom of thought they wanted.[2]

A further group of intellectuals was led by Oswald Mosley who resigned from the Labour Party in 1931 (when the Labour Cabinet refused to adopt his scheme for a planned economy) to found the New Party. Three years later Mosley's socialism turned more towards the National Socialism of Hitler's Germany, and he founded the British Union of Fascists. Its 20,000 members were to be recognized by their black shirts and high leather boots, and their actions were at first applauded, not by Socialists, but by some Conservatives who saw in Fascism an alternative to Communism — perhaps the only alternative on the continent of Europe. However, their violence

---

[1] C. Hamilton, *Modern England* (1938) quoted by ibid., p. 179.
[2] See S. King-Hall, *Three Dictators*.

and their demonstrations reduced their support, and the Public Order Act of 1936 which prevented their meetings taking place ended the movement's attempt to become a powerful political party.

The attitude of Mosley and the Fascists, however, could not be so easily overcome, especially their hatred of the Jewish race. Perhaps nothing illustrates this better than the answer David Low got, when he questioned a follower of Mosley about why the Jews were worse than other people and began by asking ' "about the thousands of secret Jewish spies pouring into Britain". He [the Fascist] had already put me to a lot of trouble investigating a story he had sent me about the landing of two thousand Jews on given dates at Southampton. His brother had actually seen them disembark. The official view, however, was that it was six hundred Czechs. . . . He gave me the story again with all the trimmings. "Official records don't tally with your story," I said. "There are plenty of Jews in the Civil Service to doctor the records," he replied. "You think your brother would know a Jew when he saw one?" I asked. "You can always tell them," he cried. "Look," I said, "there are two Jews sitting in this room right now. Point 'em out to me." He pointed out the Club's most distinguished Scotsman and a Welsh divine in mufti. We passed to his sweeping assertion that Jews were bad citizens. "Well now, that should be capable of proof," I said. "Criminal records, I suppose. What have you got?" He passed that over and went on to tell me that 95 per cent of the brothels in Berlin were run by Jews. "Now that is very interesting," I said. "So neat. From what police files did you get that figure?" "You don't get figures like that from police files," he replied. "Well, where did you get them?" I asked. "You have reliable friends who checked up? Am I to assume that you went around yourself?" He was insulted. "I am not accustomed to having my word doubted," says he, trembling. "You are trying to convince me without evidence," says I. "I could never convince you," says he, "because you are a Jew". His voice throbbed with passion. I looked into his eye and caught a glint of red madness.'[1]

[1] *Low's Autobiography*, pp. 297–298.

The intellectuals of the Left felt just as strongly about political matters as the Fascists did about Jews. How, then, did the political parties of the time react to the new interest shown in politics in the inter-war years? In what state were they to satisfy this enthusiasm for politics?

The fate of the Labour Party left many of the Left intellectuals with a feeling of failure and it is hardly surprising that some of them turned to extremes. They saw the Conservatives, the party which stood for tradition and which believed it was its right to govern because of its supporters' wealth and possessions, win election after election, although they seemed to offer little that was positive in the way of policy for the future. In 1922 Bonar Law did not do much more to canvass support than to say that 'the nation's first need is, in every walk of life, to get on with its own work, with the minimum of interference at home and of disturbance abroad'.[1] He was rewarded with five and a half million votes, 345 seats and an overall majority of 77.

On consideration it seems likely that many people voted Conservative out of hatred for Lloyd George or fear of a Labour Government. In any case the Conservatives were the only united party before the public, and the state of the Liberals and of Labour provided a sad contrast. Even after Bonar Law's and Baldwin's failure to help the country's economic position in 1922–23, the Conservatives still remained the largest single party in Parliament. The following year they gained 419 out of 615 seats in the General Election and remained in power till 1929. They did even better in 1931 when there were 473 Conservatives elected. It was thus that they dominated the National Governments after they were formed to deal with the economic crisis of 1931. And it seemed that the electorate was so well satisfied with Baldwin's performance that in 1935 he was returned to power again, this time with 432 supporters.

Yet the performance of the Conservatives was by no means as satisfactory as these majorites would suggest. The failure of any inter-war government to tackle Britain's economic troubles has already been shown,[2] and, being in power longer than any

[1] Quoted by A. J. P. Taylor, op. cit., p. 196. [2] See Chapter 3.

other party, the Conservatives must take the greater part of the blame. Nor should the Conservatives' majorities lead us to think that even at the time there was real satisfaction with their handling of two extremely important problems: the treatment of the poor, especially the unemployed, and the conduct of foreign affairs. In these two spheres there was gross mismanagement, which on the one hand might have led to civil disorder — the Hunger Marches for instance — and on the other did actually lead to the Second World War. We have seen how the public reacted to the economic and political problems; we can now turn to see how public opinion was affected by England's policy towards the rest of the world.

The basis of international understanding in these years was the League of Nations,[1] but unfortunately the League was an assembly of governments — and not even of all governments at that. The withdrawal of the USA and the exclusion at first of Germany and Russia meant that it got off to a bad start. In its first years it provided a useful centre where minor disputes could be settled, but major problems were unlikely to be solved since the great powers could agree on no plan of mutual military assistance to enforce their decisions. England's Labour government rejected such a scheme in 1924 and the Conservatives acted similarly a year later.

Nevertheless from the middle twenties foreign secretaries usually attended meetings of the League's Council, the first to attend being Austen Chamberlain. This increased its standing in the public's mind. In fact many ordinary people as well as idealists pinned their hopes for peace on the success of the League, and local branches of the League of Nations Union had been set up as early as 1919 in places as different as Droitwich, a spa for retired Conservatives, and Derby, a town with strong radical traditions and sympathies. In Derby one of the first meetings stressed that the League was not a mere utopian idea, but that it 'was absolutely essential to prevent the suicide of the human race'.[2] Disarmament became the central

---

[1] For full details of the League of Nations see Pauline Bloncourt, *The Embattled Peace 1919–1939.*

[2] *Derby Mercury*, 7th March 1919.

point of the beliefs of many League of Nations Union supporters. For many clear-thinking people it was linked with the need to provide enough strength to support 'collective security' through the use of the machinery of the League of Nations. To others, who perhaps did not think quite so clearly, disarmament was a kind of substitute for collective security. There were also many people who believed that building up national arms led to an 'arms race', and so to war. And as well as these hidden divisions among the disarmers, one wonders whether enough people really believed fully in the League. The attitude of Colonel Blimp, the self-contradictory Conservative of Low's cartoons, was perhaps, all too frequent: 'Gad, sir, Mr. Lansbury is right. The League of Nations should insist on peace — except, of course, in the event of war.'[1]

The work of the League gave the public few reasons to idolize it. Indeed, after initial enthusiasm many people wavered in their belief in the League. We can see how public opinion changed if we look at the main crises with which the League had to deal in the thirties — the economic crisis, the Sino-Japanese war, the problem of the re-emergence and rearmament of Germany, the Italian invasion of Abyssinia, the Spanish Civil War and the annexations of Austria and Czechoslovakia.

These were all problems with which England was concerned for they all threatened to upset the peace of Europe, if not the world. Unfortunately England's governments of the inter-war years never really made up their minds how active a part they should play in either the League of Nations or Europe. Public opinion, too, was divided and it seems likely that the governments mirrored the public's views faithfully. There was still a feeling, probably coming from traditions of the nineteenth century, that Britain should play only a small part in Europe, mainly concerning the settling of disputes. This may have been behind her seeming desertion of France over the Rhineland problem.

Originally the Treaty of Versailles had given France a joint Anglo-American guarantee of military help if Germany attacked France, but, when the US Senate did not ratify the

[1] *Low's Autobiography*, p. 267.

24. (*left to right*) Anthony Eden, M. Laval and Baron Aloisi in informal talks between League of Nations meetings during the Abyssinian Crisis

treaty, England took it that her part of this bargain was cancelled too. Yet England and France were the only two major countries with any real belief in peace or in the Treaty of Versailles. Japan and Italy, the two other major powers, were lukewarm in their support, as they both had plans for territorial expansion and aggression of the kind that would conflict with the principles of the League. The maintenance of peace and of the League as a centre of world consultation was thus very much in the hands of France and England. France who had known two German invasions within almost a generation — in 1870 and 1914 — saw in the Treaty and the League her sole hope of safety. England, traditionally standing aside from European matters, was in favour of the League as long as she was not expected to do anything active. The result was to all intents and purposes the collapse of the victorious alliance of 1918 and the creation of a situation in which the crises of the late twenties and thirties led to the Second World War.[1]

One of the first of these crises was the attack made on China by Japan.[2] In 1931 Japanese troops had entered Manchuria and had completed its conquest by 1932. Japan would not admit aggression and in March 1933 resigned from the League and continued her expansion into China. This was the first really

[1] See H. Browne, *The Second World War.*
[2] See Hugh Higgins, *From Warlords to Red Star.*

important reverse suffered by the League and the success with which Japan ignored the League probably gave encouragement to other countries in the thirties in their plans for aggressive expansion.

Britain's attitude seems to have been that, although the Japanese had acted wrongly, their action must be forgotten and perhaps forgiven for the sake of peace. There appears to have been a widespread fear that defiance of Japan might lead to a general war, and that Sino-Japanese hostility — in any case a long way away — was a passing problem which would eventually solve itself. Here was one of the contradictions of the time: every country talked about peace through collective security and helping each other, but refused to act together to prevent aggression which was such a threat to peace. Britain and most other nations shrank from problems which might involve them in war.

The fact that the Sino-Japanese problem proved to be anything but a passing problem should have been brought home to Britain in the later thirties, for in 1937 Japan renewed her advance into China, taking Peking and Tientsin. China appealed to the League for help but none was forthcoming. In 1938 the Council of the League expressed sympathy for China and left it to individual countries to help China as they thought fit. Only Russia provided China with any practical help.

By the late thirties the great powers were immersed in the problems of Europe itself. As early as 1933 the disarmament conference had reached deadlock and on the pretext of this failure Germany had resigned from the League, at the same time denouncing the Locarno Pacts which had guaranteed existing Franco-German boundaries and demilitarized the Rhineland. Was this to be treated by England as yet another transitory problem? Apparently so, for the Hitler-led Germany[1] went on to rearm openly and with little opposition. With the question of disarmament thus temporarily closed every country was soon arming itself, making Europe unsettled and frightened. The two prevailing views can be seen clearly in Britain. On the one hand in 1932 Winston Churchill maintained that

[1] See *Three Dictators* for details of Hitler.

Germany wanted more than equal status in Europe: 'All these bands of sturdy Teutonic youths . . . are not looking for status. They are looking for weapons.' He asked for Britain to rearm.[1] On the other hand John Wilmot was said to have won his seat at East Fulham for Labour in 1933 by the votes of pacifists. This conflict of opinion was present all through the thirties and was reflected in half-hearted government policy.

Yet, as with Japan and China, the problem of Germany was to worsen in the future. And Europe, having closed its eyes at the outset, kept them closed — even when in March 1936 Hitler's troops reoccupied the Rhineland. France's government was too weak to take action and merely consulted Britain, who hid behind the consolation of Hitler's constant talk of peace and his promises that he only wanted what was in truth Germany's territory. Those who knew Hitler's Germany felt no trust in the promises made. Sir Horace Rumbold, Britain's Ambassador in Berlin, said, 'Everything shows that this Nazi revolution has brought out some of the worst characteristics in the German character, namely a mean spirit of revenge, brutality amounting in many cases to bestiality, and complete ruthlessness.' Even if French and British leaders had been determined to fight Germany, it is doubtful whether they would have had much support, so determined were many people for peace. It was this attitude which backed the so-called policy of appeasement. It was in many ways short-sighted — peace for the present at the cost of an insecure future — though it is difficult to see what alternative policy could have been followed at a time when England's and France's supply of armaments was so low.

Nor was Hitler's Germany the only problem confronting England in the thirties. Indeed Hitler used the confusion caused by other problems to pursue his aims. Thus at the time of the Italo–Abyssinian War he reoccupied the Rhineland. Italy, since 1922 led by Mussolini,[2] attacked Abyssinia in December 1934 and the following year annexed it. Abyssinia, a member of the League, appealed to the Council, which declared Italy the

[1] See *An Old and a Young Leader*
[2] See *Three Dictators* for Mussolini.

aggressor and asked members of the League to apply economic sanctions against her. The USA joined this plan to some extent, but Austria, Hungary, Albania and Switzerland refused. Italy was supplied with most necessary goods, while Britain learnt, as she was to learn again in the sixties over Rhodesia, how hard it was to apply economic sanctions effectively without the use of force. There was little likelihood of force being used against Italy in 1935 or even in 1936 when Italian expansion was even more blatant. Italy moreover reacted to the sanctions by resigning from the League in 1937. There was no denying that Mussolini had been successful in defying the League and, as in the case of Japan, other countries were encouraged. Britain appeared, through her inaction, to be less involved in Europe than ever. The opinion seemed to be that it was unsafe to quarrel with Mussolini as well as Hitler — better divide them from one another and perhaps deal with one at a time. 'We shall have to compromise with Mussolini, for we can never compromise securely or even live safely with Dictator Major (Hitler), if we are at loggerheads with Dictator Minor (Mussolini).' These were the words, no doubt typical, of Sir Robert Vansittart, Permanent Under Secretary at the Foreign Office. The British public suffered from the same weak, wishful thinking — that two dictators could not possibly get on with each other — and in this theory they were joined by the French politicians of the time. The British and French Ministers wavered fatally between two policies: keeping the friendship of Italy as a help against Germany and preventing aggression by either dictator. The unhappy result was that Mussolini gained both the loot from his aggression and also formed a firm alliance with Hitler, the Rome–Berlin *Axis* as it was called. Later this alliance was joined by Japan.

Another fatal weakness and division of both politicians and public opinion concerned Russia. Many Conservative leaders were inclined to think that Communism and Soviet dictatorship was the worst threat of all.[1] To them even Hitler had his uses as a bulwark against Russia. On the other hand many left-wing intellectuals idealized and idolized Russia, while ordinary

[1] See *Three Dictators* for Stalin.

people who thought about the matter remained undecided. Again the result was wavering and indecision. Russia joined the League in 1934, and for a time there was perhaps real hope that her power would supply the strength needed for collective security in Eastern Europe. But this did not happen, and, when German aggression grew, the Western countries of Europe and Soviet Russia were unable to follow a common policy.

These doubts, divisions, self-deceptions and fears were to a great extent fused together at the time of the Spanish Civil War. The peace-loving people of Europe watched with growing horror exactly what the next European war would be like, for it seems that Germany, Italy and perhaps Russia used Spain as the trial ground for the latest developments in warfare. And when we look at the effects on Spain of the Civil War, we can appreciate why Europe hesitated to embark on war. We can also see why it was the Spanish Civil War that caused the greatest outcry of the inter-war years. It was the crisis which resulted in one of the greatest out-pourings of emotion in modern times.

There had already been a play about the next European war called *Idiot's Delight* in which the emotions of those who opposed war were shown: 'They're all talking about security. They're all jittery. So they get bigger cannons and sharper bayonets. And that makes them more jittery. . . . I'll tell you what else you can do in these tragic circumstances. You can refuse to fight.'[1] The fighting in Spain brought some people's feelings to a climax. It also brought the views of many intellectuals to the test, for here in Spain was the chance for them to support their words by actions. Such poets as W. H. Auden went to Spain, like the crusaders of medieval times, to fight for their beliefs and to found a new state:

'What's your proposal? To build the just city? I will.
I agree. Or is it the suicide pact, the romantic
    Death? Very well, I accept, for
I am your choice, your decision. Yes I am Spain.'

This close identification of some English people with the Left

[1] Quoted by R. Graves and A. Hodge, op. cit., p. 417.

in Spain must not make us forget that it was first and foremost a Spanish tragedy. The Spaniards were in fact settling old quarrels of their own and into this quarrel came the rest of Europe — Germany and Italy, the Fascist countries of Europe, on one side, the Russians, Communists and the International Brigade on the other. It was this intervention of Europe which made the war look exclusively one between Fascists and Communists, between Right and Left. In actual fact after the collapse of the Spanish monarchy in 1931 a republic was declared under General Sanjurjo. The weakness of the republic meant that extremists on both Right and Left struggled for power so that the country was plunged into Civil War.

The Conservative republicans — the Right or the Nation-alists — led by Gil Robles and Calvo Sotelo, had the support of the Spanish Foreign Legion and tried to gain control of the extreme Left areas of Spain, the Asturias district for instance, by force. The weak government was unable to control the Right and open fighting broke out in May 1936. Two months later Sotelo was murdered and leadership of the Right was taken over by General Franco. Soon the Right were in league with Mussolini and Hitler, so that by 1937 there were 80,000 Italian and 30,000 German troops in Spain. The legitimate government now supported by the Socialists, Basque Nationalists and Communists — the Left — held Madrid and were backed to a lesser extent by Russia who provided arms, guns, tanks and planes.

On the whole Britain sympathized with the Left and was hostile to Franco's Spain, but no definite help was sent since Britain, almost alone, stood by the Non-Intervention Agree-ment signed with Italy, Germany and Russia in 1936. The war was particularly odious and savage as perhaps only civil war can be. Guernica, for instance, with its 7,000 inhabitants, was wiped out and something of the horror of the war can be seen in Picasso's picture inspired by this episode. Picasso shows a mother screaming powerlessly upwards as her child is killed, surrounded by agonized faces of women, and so expresses the anguish of an unparallelled disaster. Indeed all Picasso's work of this period is intense with foreboding — 'Cat Devouring a

Bird', for instance — as if he knew that soon war would not be confined to Spain.

The war ended officially in March 1939 with Franco's victory over the Left, though many Spaniards refused to recognize the victory. It was in some ways a victory for European Fascism over Communism and probably emboldened the Fascist states of Europe, Germany and Italy, to speed up their aggression in other parts of the world. The victory was also a great blow to the intellectuals of the Left — the poets and novelists such as Spender, Auden and MacNeice for instance — and to many who had joined the 2,762 British volunteers in the International Brigade. While the war was in progress their devotion never wavered, although 543 were killed and 1,763 wounded. But once war ended, the futility of war and the desperation of their own position became obvious. Their high ideals had failed to be put into practice and they had seen how ideals had to be compromised when it was a matter of fighting a war.

Yet at least one lesson had been learnt by Britain, for the Spanish Civil War taught both Socialists and Conservatives to hate Fascism. It was probably to some extent due to this that, when the Second World War broke out, Britain was able on the whole to enter the War united against Germany. For gradually people began to realize, at first with incredulous despair and then with mounting anger and courage, that Hitler was the main challenge to peace.[1] When in March 1938 Austria had been absorbed into Germany, many British people comforted themselves that not all Austrians disapproved of Hitler, despite the stories of German and Austrian Jewish and democratic refugees. Chamberlain's appeasement policy had in fact strong public support. Not everyone agreed of course. Eden resigned as Foreign Secretary over disagreements on Italian policy. Churchill continued to warn the country of the dangers of Nazi Germany.

After the seizure of Austria events moved swiftly. A rude awakening awaited some of those who had condoned it, when, seven months later, Hitler annexed the Sudeten district of

[1] See Harry Browne, *The Second World War.*

Czechoslovakia, this time with the full approval of Britain and France. Hitler was determined to gain Czech territory; Britain under Chamberlain, and France under Daladier, were determined on peace. Hence there was made the famous Munich Agreement in September, whereby Germany was allowed to annex part of Czechoslovakia peacefully. This was the greatest extent to which Chamberlain's policy of appeasement could go. He really did believe that this arrangement would satisfy Hitler. He felt that his personal contact with Hitler was some guarantee of good faith. He also was convinced that the state of Britain's armaments precluded the use of force for the time being.

Chamberlain's policy received much support and acclamation. *The Times* even managed to make the agreement appear morally right, forgetting that England had guaranteed Czech boundaries by signing the Treaty of Versailles. Chamberlain himself received 40,000 letters, most of them showing sincere thanks and relief that war, as they thought, had been averted. On the other hand, Duff Cooper resigned in protest and, on behalf of the Labour Party, Clement Attlee said: 'We have been unable to go in for carefree rejoicing. We have felt that we are in the midst of a tragedy. We have felt humiliation. This has not been a victory for reason and humanity. It has been a victory for brute force. . . . We have seen . . . a gallant, civilized and democratic people betrayed and handed over to a ruthless despotism.'

It is, of course, too easy for us to look back and criticize Chamberlain for the Munich agreement. What should not be forgotten is that it gave immense relief at the time, not only in Britain but also in France. Many people believed wholeheartedly that, as Chamberlain put it, 'This is the second time in our history that there has come back from Germany to Downing Street peace with honour. I believe it is peace in our time.'

Not everyone, as we have seen, agreed with Chamberlain and his policy. Gilbert Murray, a leader of the League of Nations Union, in a letter to *The Times*, hoped that 'the world can be shown that at some point somewhere Great Britain will keep her covenants and protect those who trust in her'.

That point did in fact come fairly soon, not over Czecho-slovakia, of which Germany had taken over the rest in March 1939, but over Poland. In many ways this was not so much a change of policy on Britain's part, but was the signal that rearmament had reached the state that made it possible for Britain to give guarantees to countries which might suffer from German aggression. In March Poland received such guarantees from Britain and France, and Rumania was provided for similarly in April. It was this guarantee to Poland that brought Britain and France into the Second World War. Germany attacked Poland on 1st September, but even so Britain and France held back for two days in the hope that a peaceful solution might be found.

It was in fact parliamentary and public opinion which in the end impelled Chamberlain to declare war. The experience of the Spanish Civil War and the moral outrage at the brutalities and dishonesties of Hitler made compromise no longer possible. In this time of crisis and in this culmination of instability, the divisions of the inter-war years were largely forgotten. When Churchill formed his war cabinet in May 1940, England had at last a truly national government, which not only stood a chance of winning the war with the wholehearted support it received from the country, but also made possible through its schemes of social reforms the healing of those cleavages which had been so marked between 1918 and 1939.

Bibliography

FOR PUPILS

Allen, A. B., *20th Century Britain, 1900–1950*, New Project History Series (Barrie & Rockliff, 1958)

Cootes, R. J., *The General Strike 1926*, Then & There Series (Longmans, 1964)

Crowther, J. G., *Six Great Inventors* (Hamish Hamilton, 1961)

Harston, K., *Yesterday: A History of the Time of Your Parents and Grandparents*, Understanding the Modern World Series (Allen & Unwin, 3rd ed., 1961)

McNicol, H., *Seven Inventors*, Living Names Series (Oxford University Press, 1943, 16th imp., 1965)

Priestley, H. E. and Betts, J. J., *The Momentous Years 1919–1958* (Dent, rev. ed., 1959)

Walters, D. W., *Modern Lives* (Collins, 1954)

Wymer, N., *Great Inventors*, Lives of Great Men and Women Series (Oxford University Press, 1957)

FOR TEACHERS

Blyth, R., *The Age of Illusion* (Hamish Hamilton, 1963; also Penguin)

Briggs, A., *Seebohm Rowntree* (Longmans, 1961)

Briggs, A. (Ed.), *They Saw it Happen, Book 4 1898–1945* (Blackwell, 1960)

Cecil, Viscount, *A Great Experiment* (Cape, 1941)

Feiling, K. G., *The Life of Neville Chamberlain* (Macmillan, 1946)

Graves, R. and Hodge, A., *The Long Weekend* (Four Square Books, 1965)

Hamilton, M. A., *Arthur Henderson* (Heinemann, 1938)

Lowndes, G. A. N., *The Silent Social Revolution* (Oxford University Press, 1937)

McElwee, W., *Britain's Locust Years 1918–1940* (Faber, 1962)

Montgomery, J., *The Twenties* (Allen & Unwin, 1957)

Mowat, C. L., *Britain Between the Wars 1918–1940* (Methuen, 1955)

Muggeridge, M., *The Thirties* (Collins, 1967)

Nicolson, H., *King George the Fifth* (Constable, 1953)

Percy, Lord Eustace, *Some Memories* (Eyre & Spottiswoode, 1958)

Poole, R. H., *The Picture History of Fifty Years 1900–1951* (Newnes, 1952)

Postgate, R., *George Lansbury* (Longmans, 1951)

Taylor, A. J. P., *English History 1914–1945*, Oxford History of England v. 15 (Oxford University Press, 1965)

Thomas, J. H., *My Story* (Hutchinson, 1937)

Thompson, D., *England in the Twentieth Century* Pelican History of England, Vol. 9 (Penguin, 1965)

Index